# Impressions

Stress relieving coloring pages for adults with an oil paint style

## Illustrated by Lonn Hunter

Dedicated to Teryl, without which my life would have little meaning

Arno River, Florence, Italy

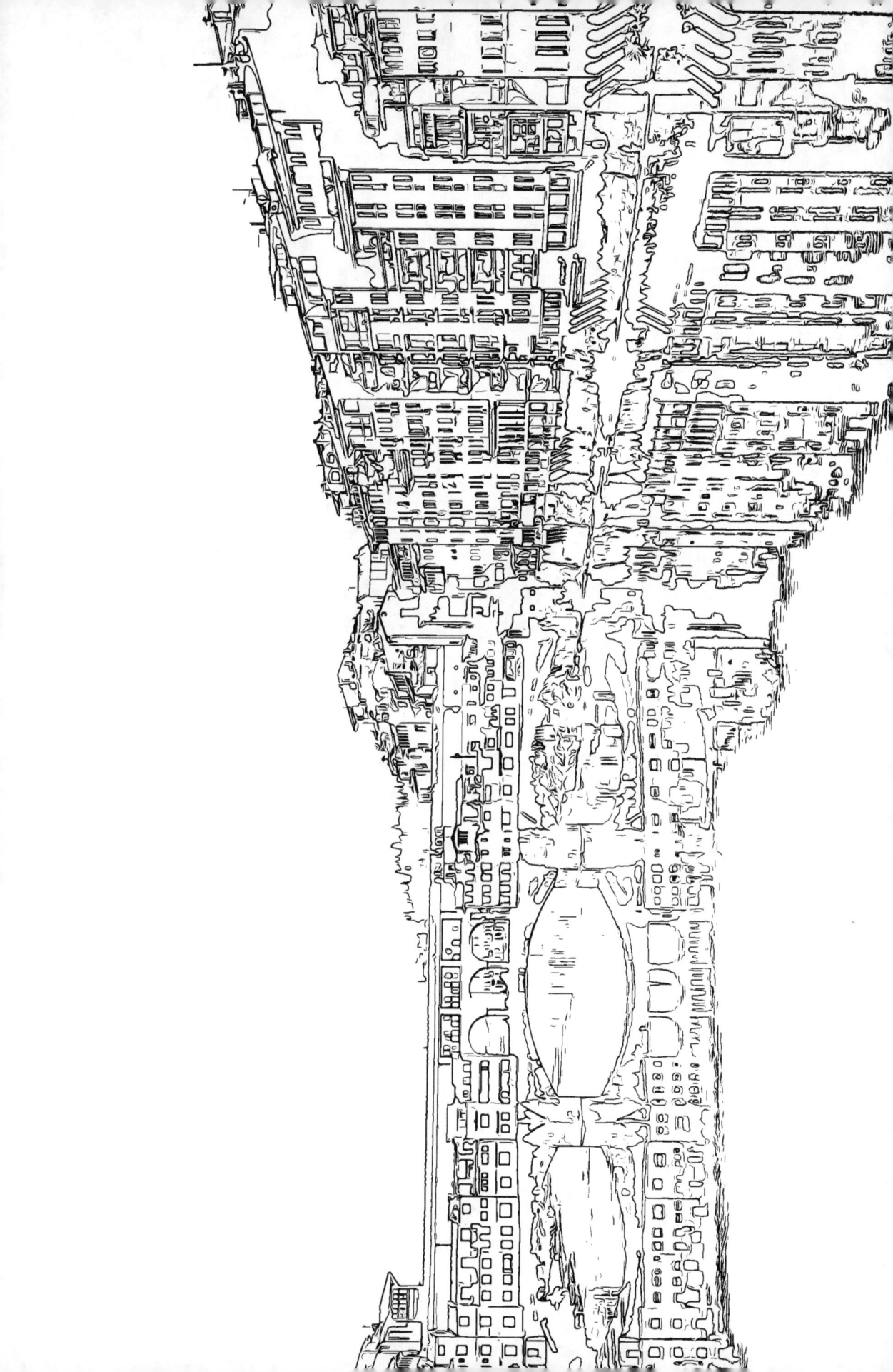

Benedictine Abby of Maria Laach

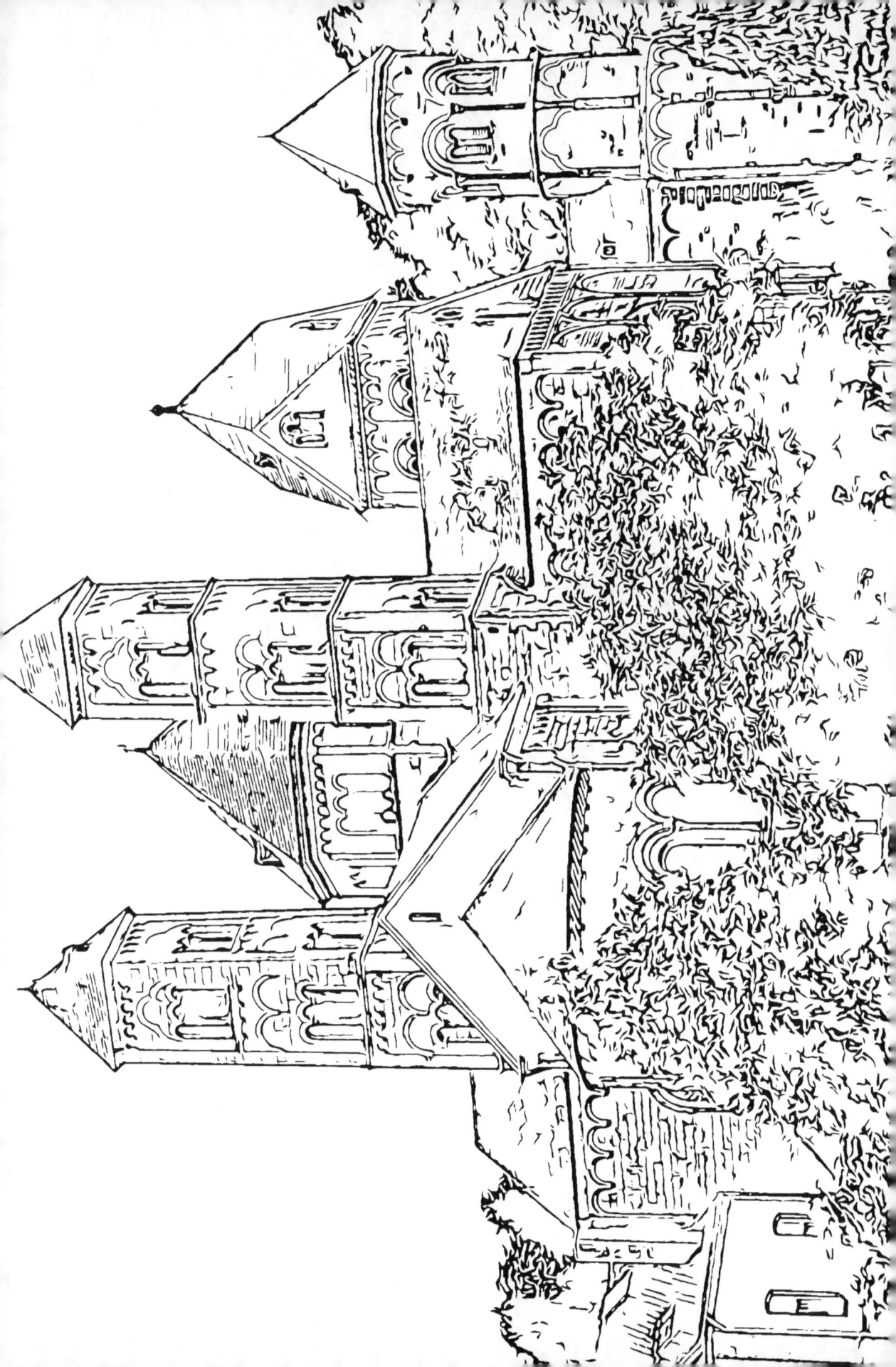

# Boat on the beach

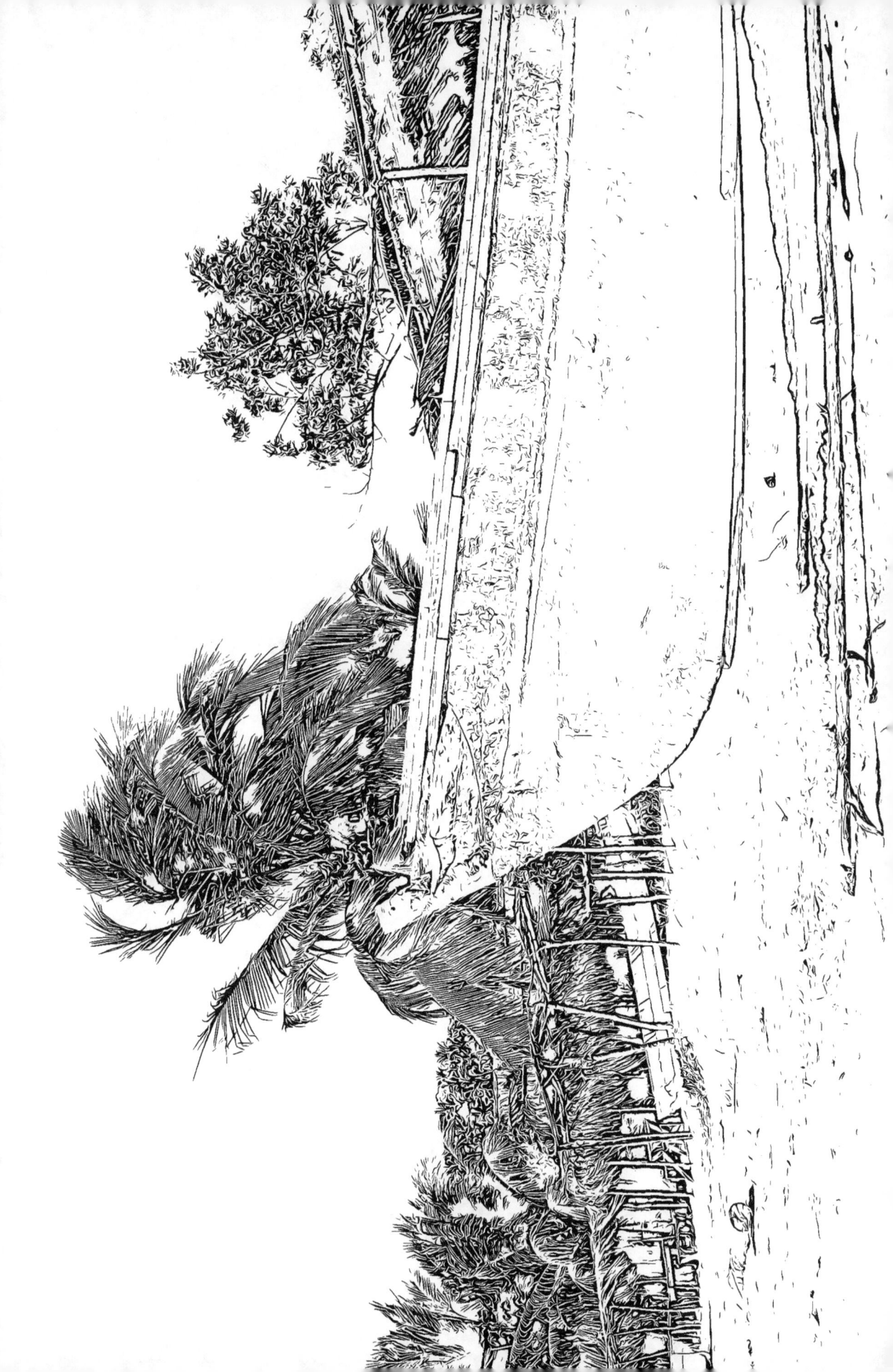

Bridge in Brittany, France

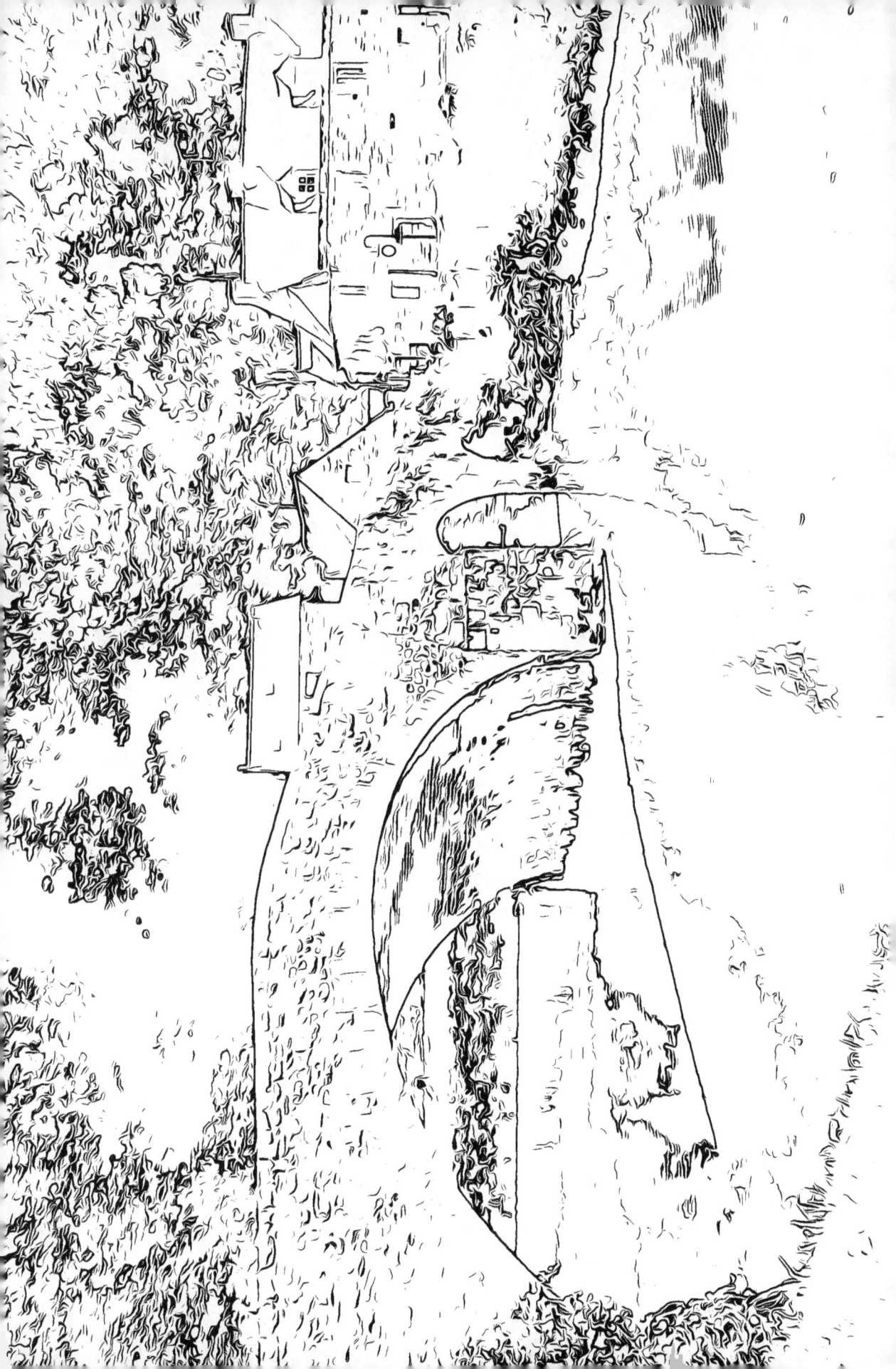

# Butterfly

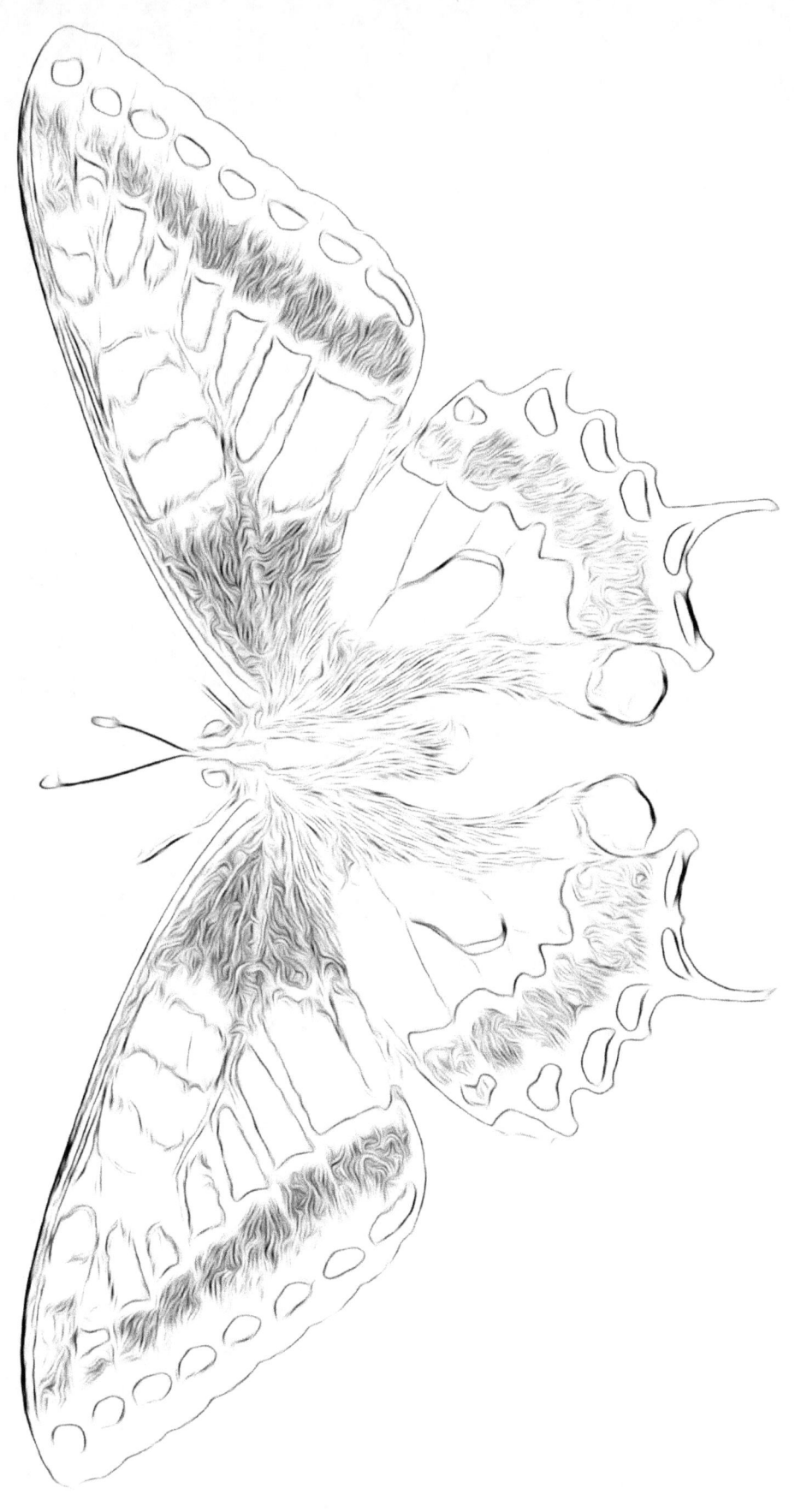

Cambridge, Massachusetts, USA

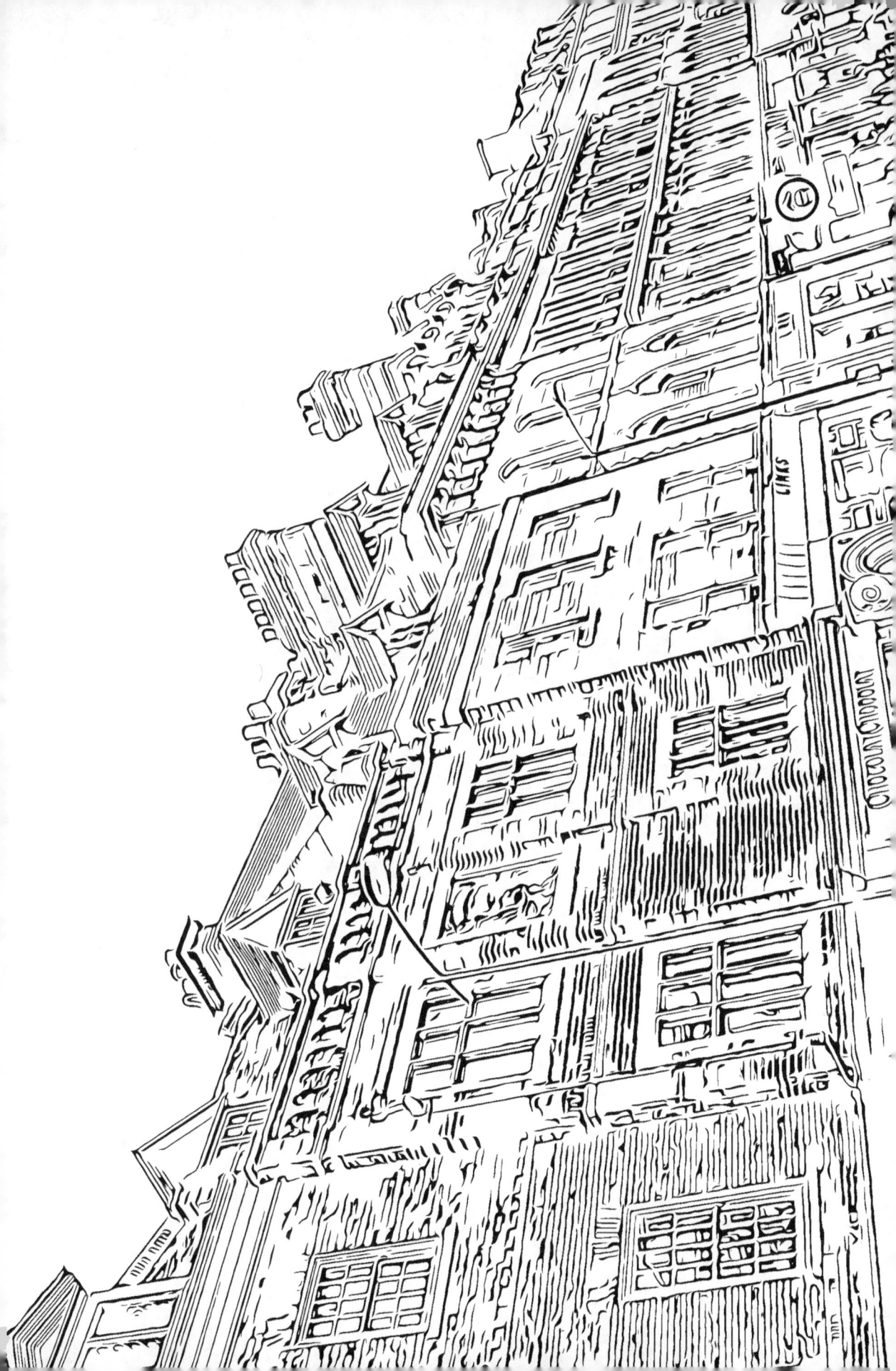

Celle, Lower Saxony, Germany

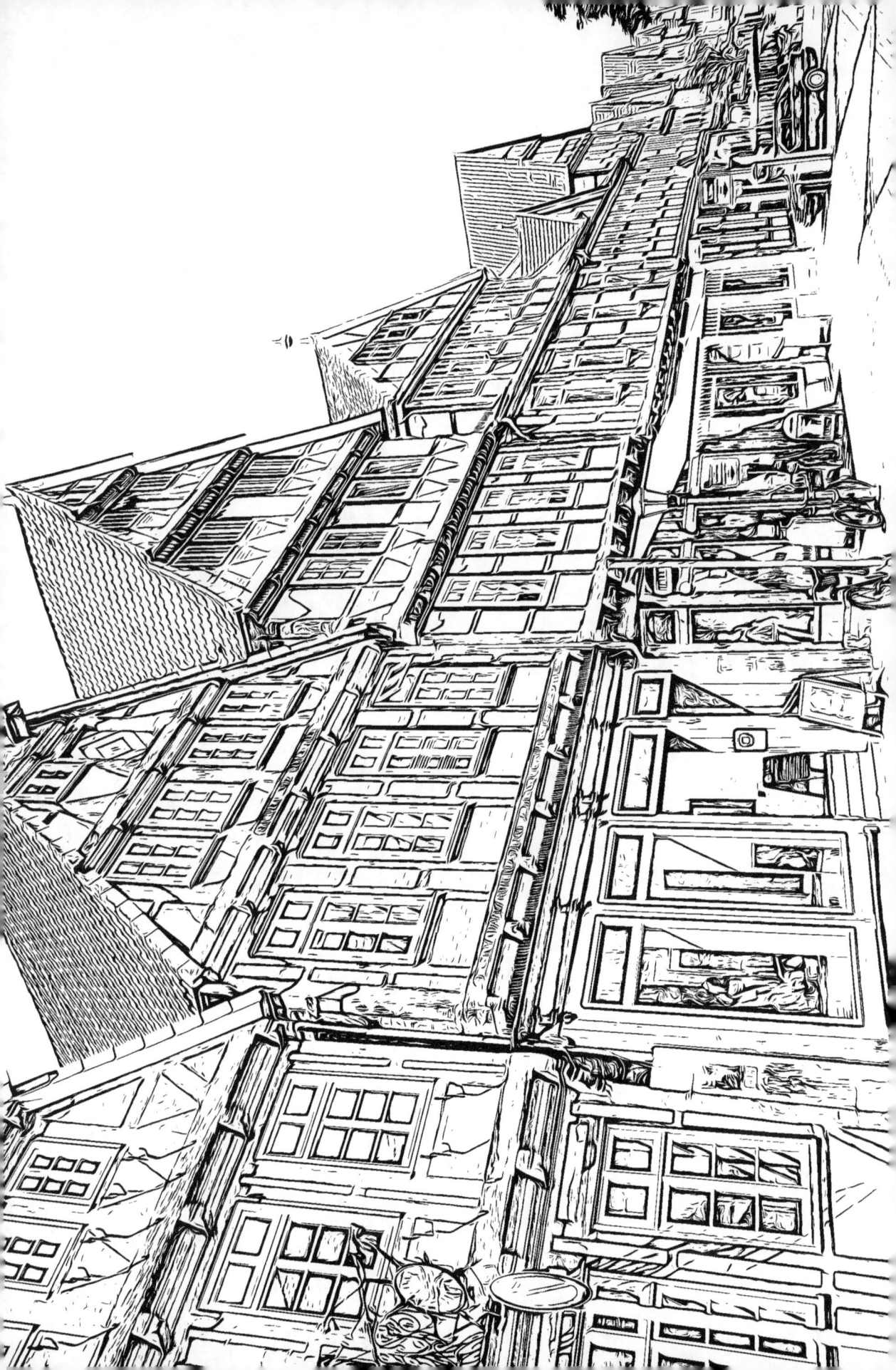

Cinque Terre, Italy

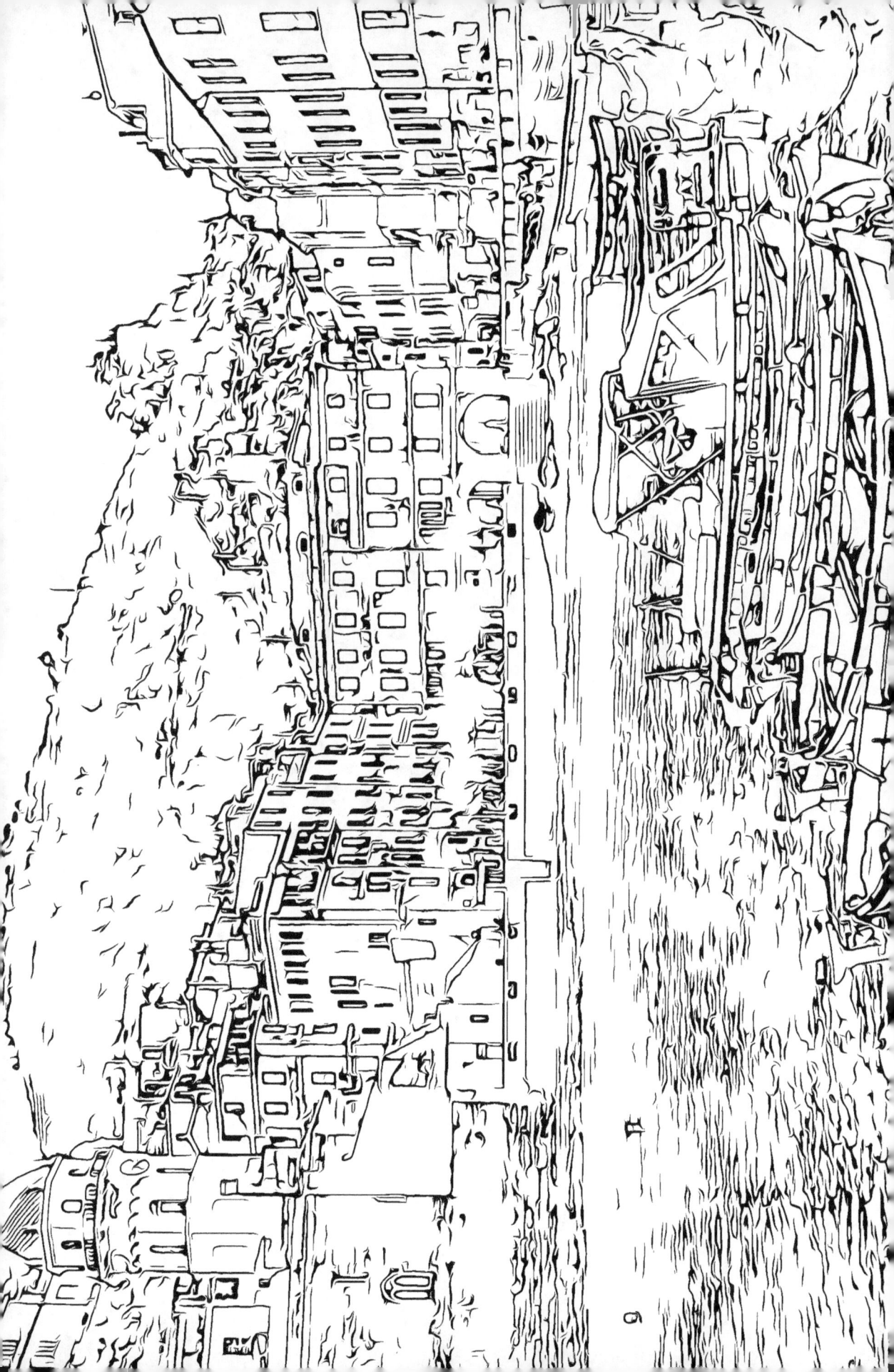

Collesuem, Rome, Italy

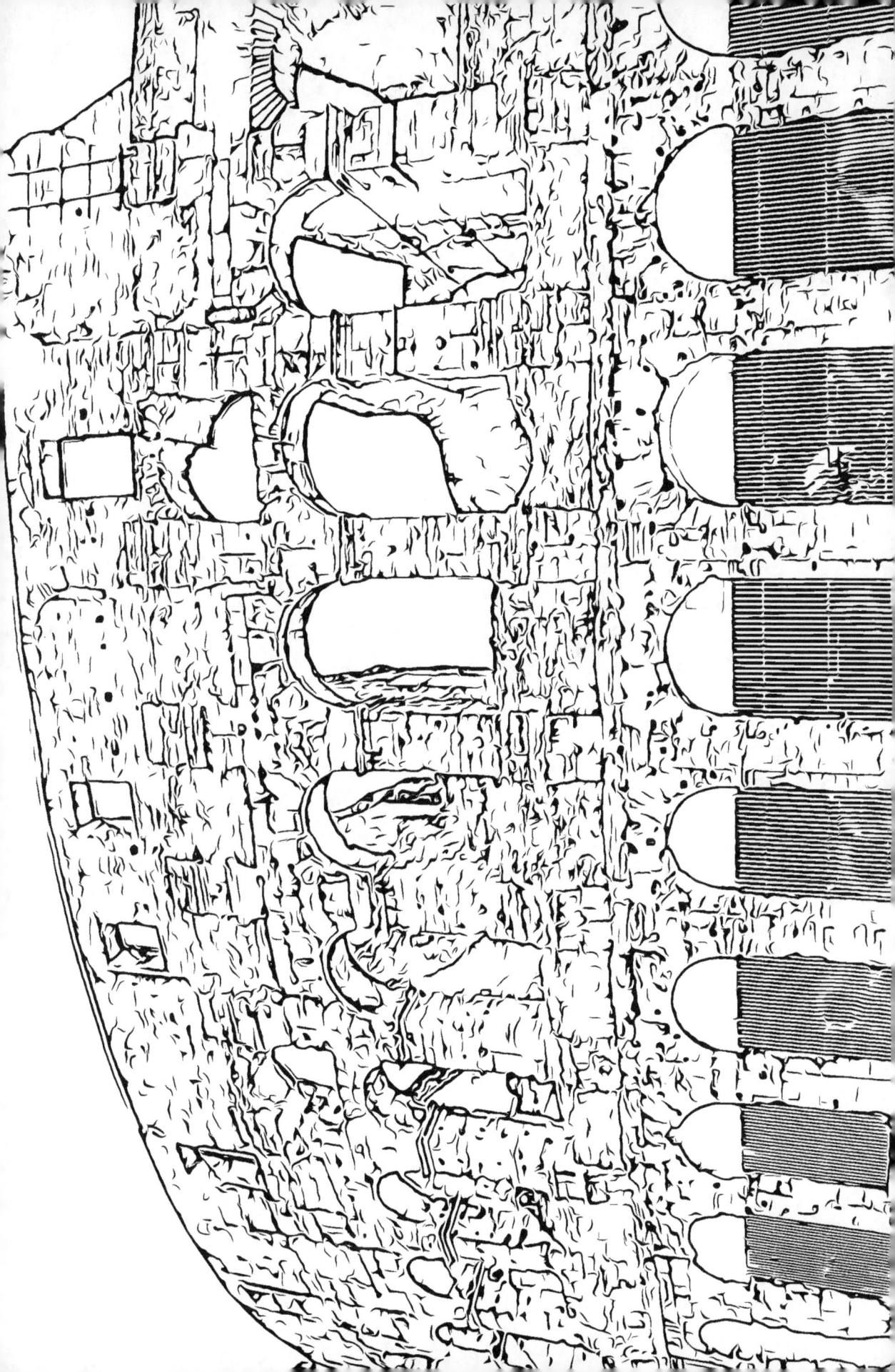

Cottage in Cornwall, England

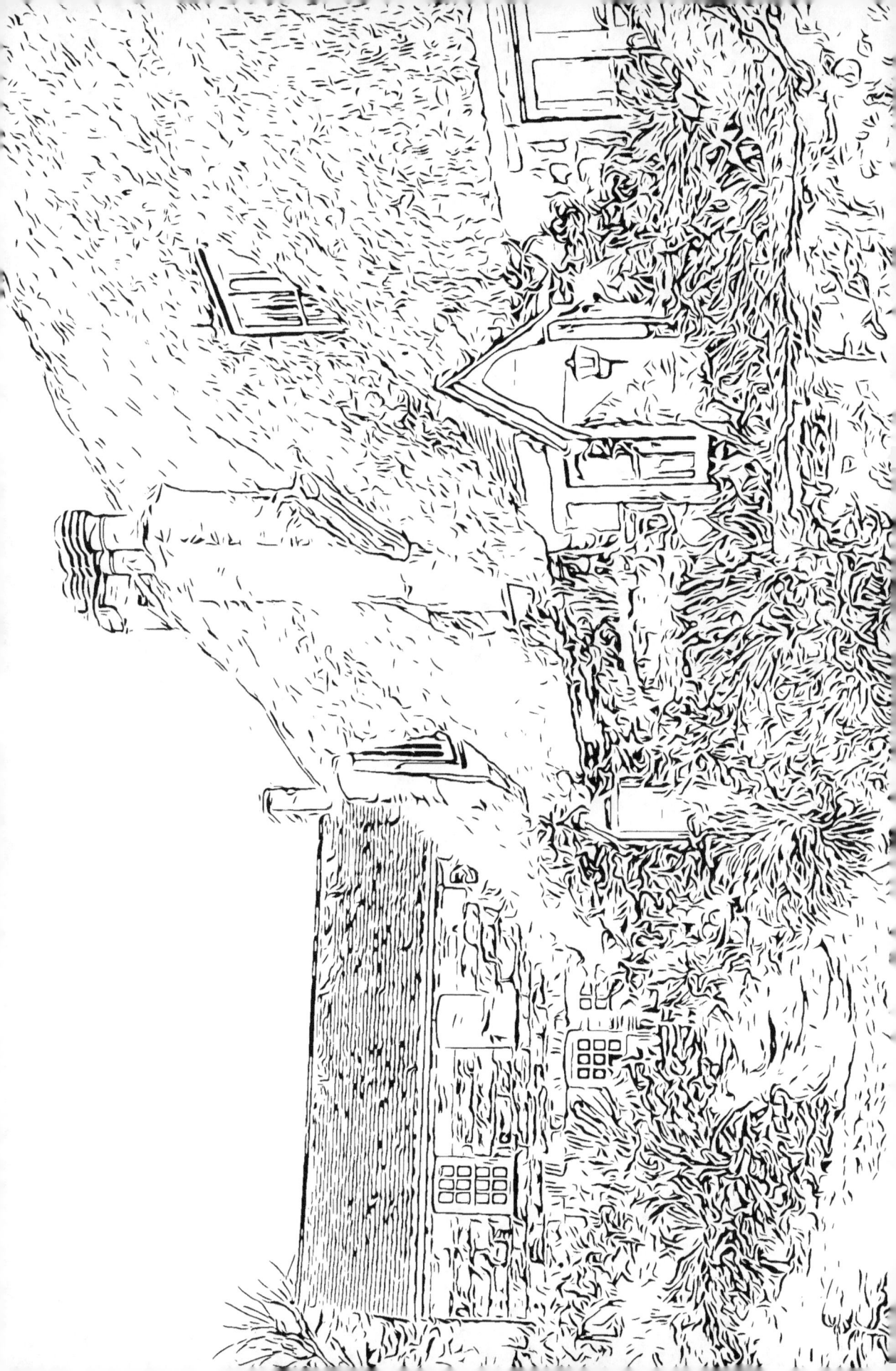

Cinque Terre, Italy

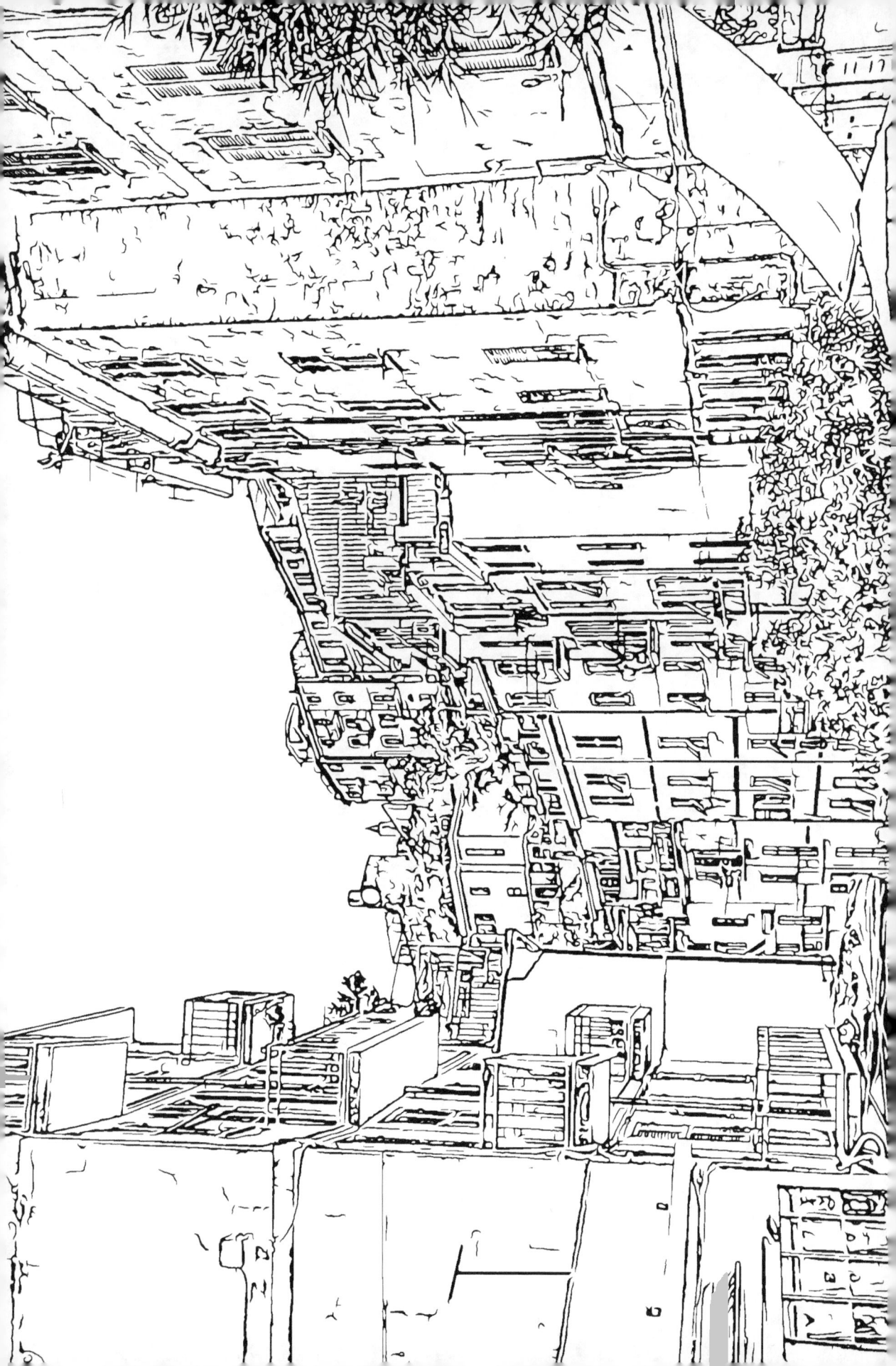

Church, location unknown

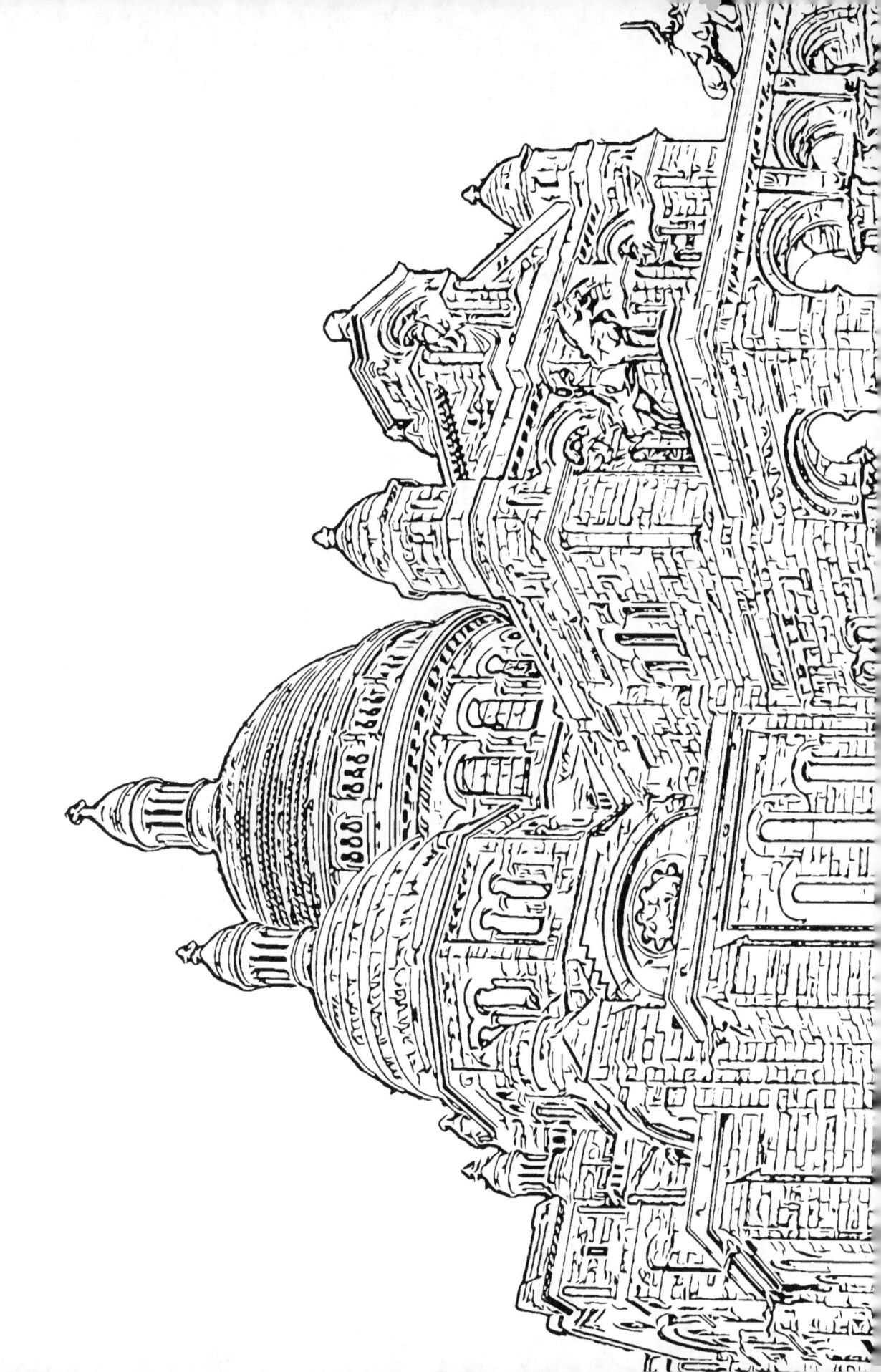

# Church Window

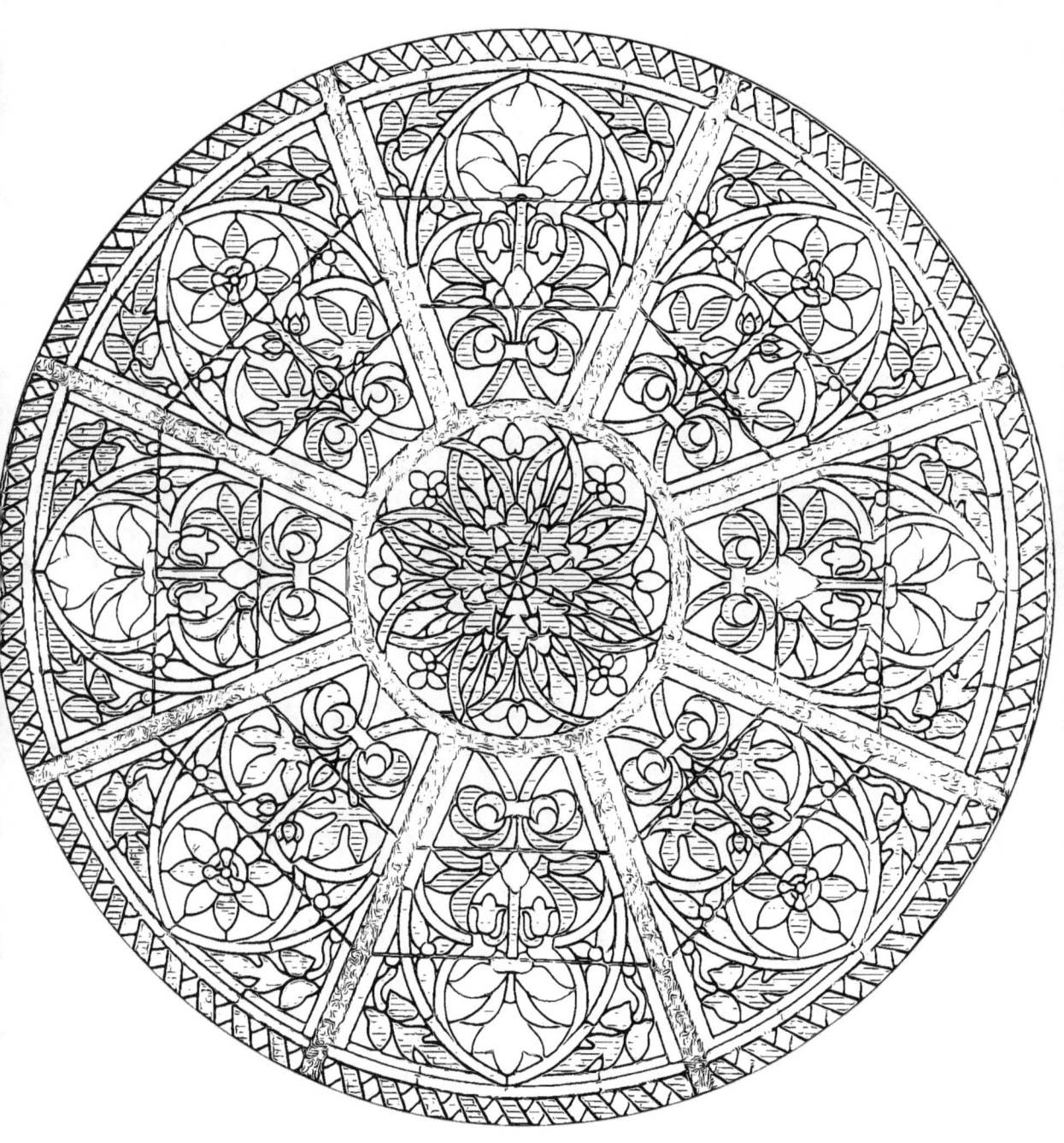

Cuomo, Italy

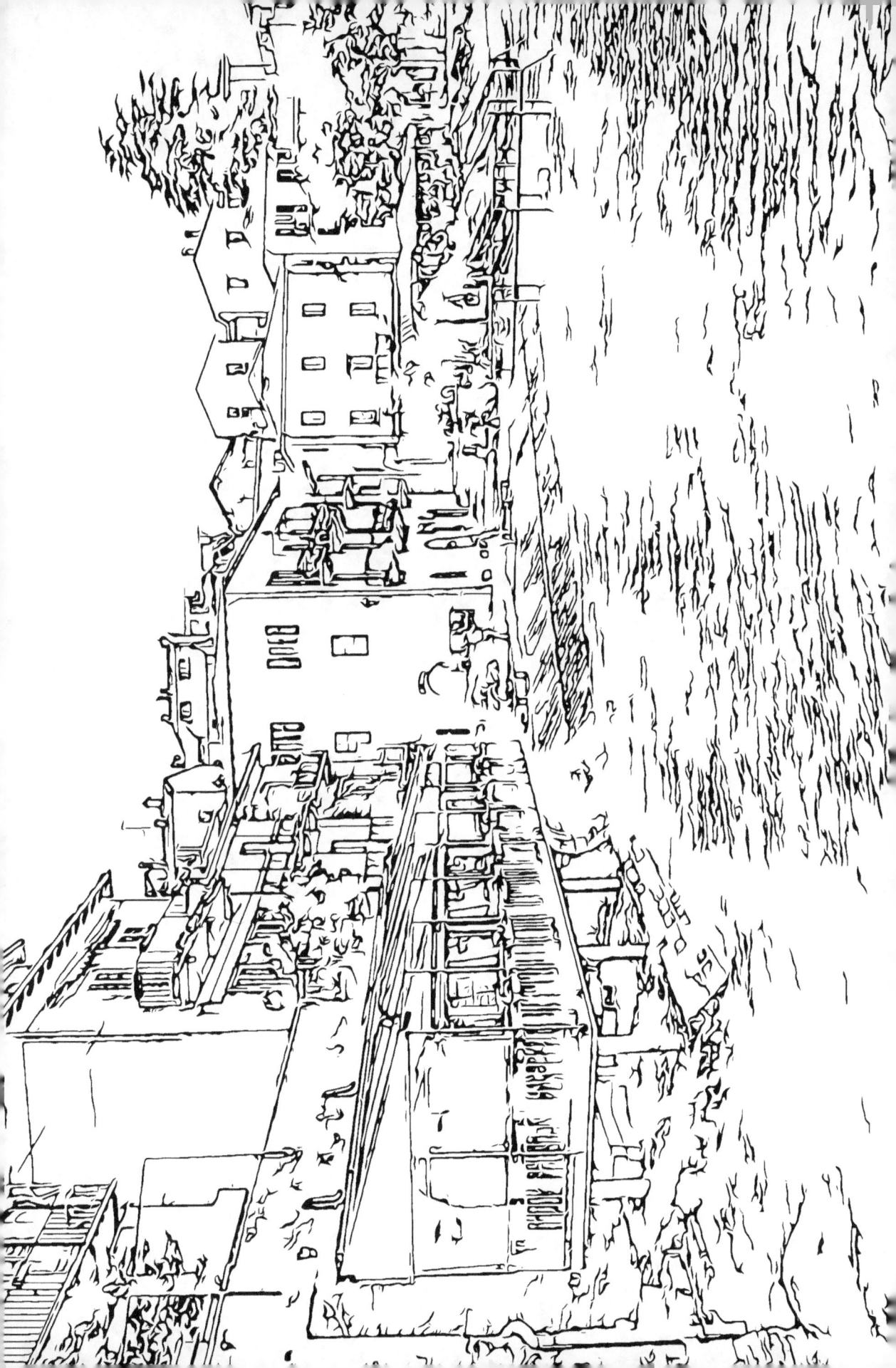

Fishing boats in dry dock

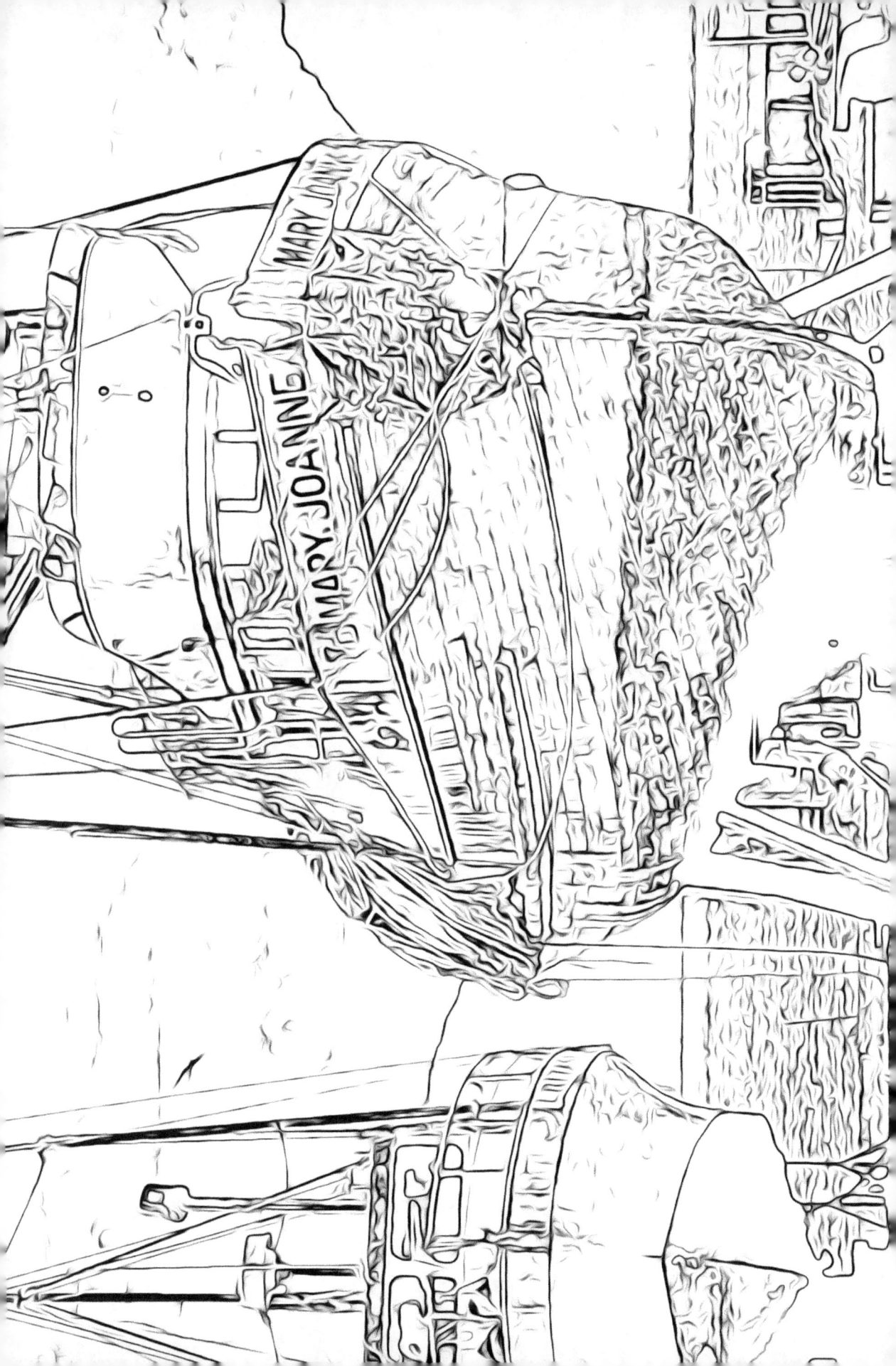

Hluboka, South Bohemia

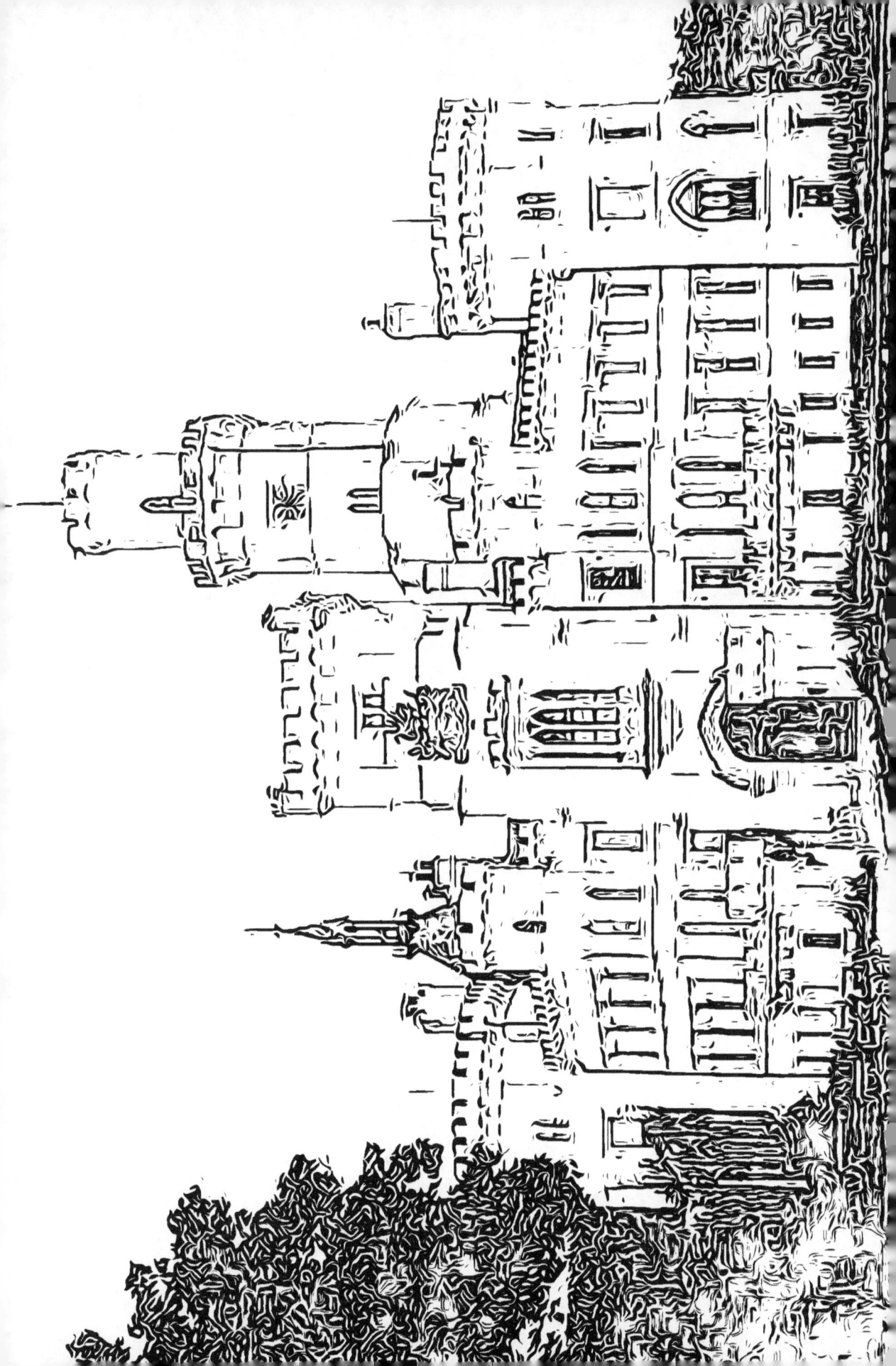

# South Bohemia

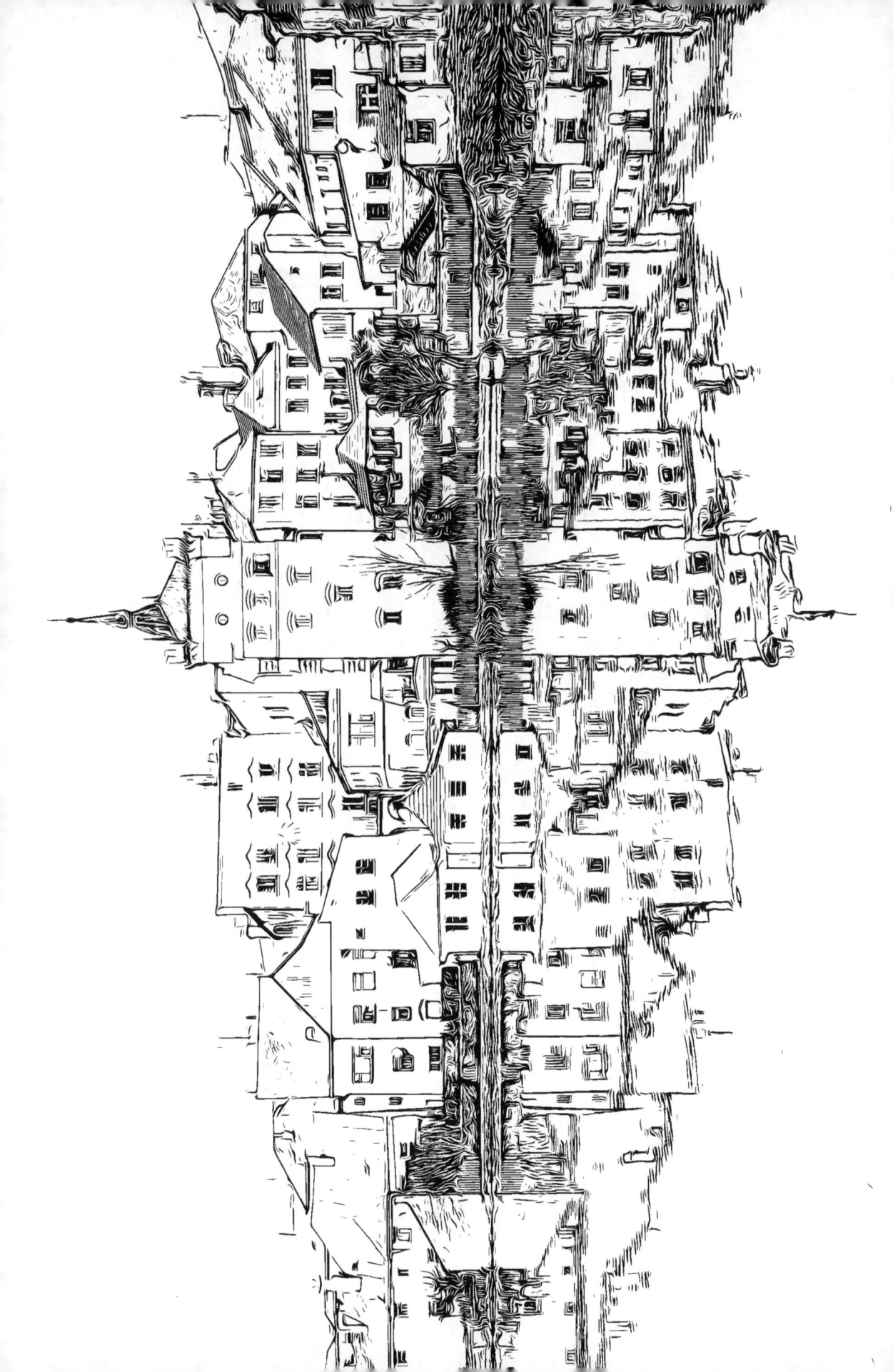

Langforden Church, Lower South Saxoney, France

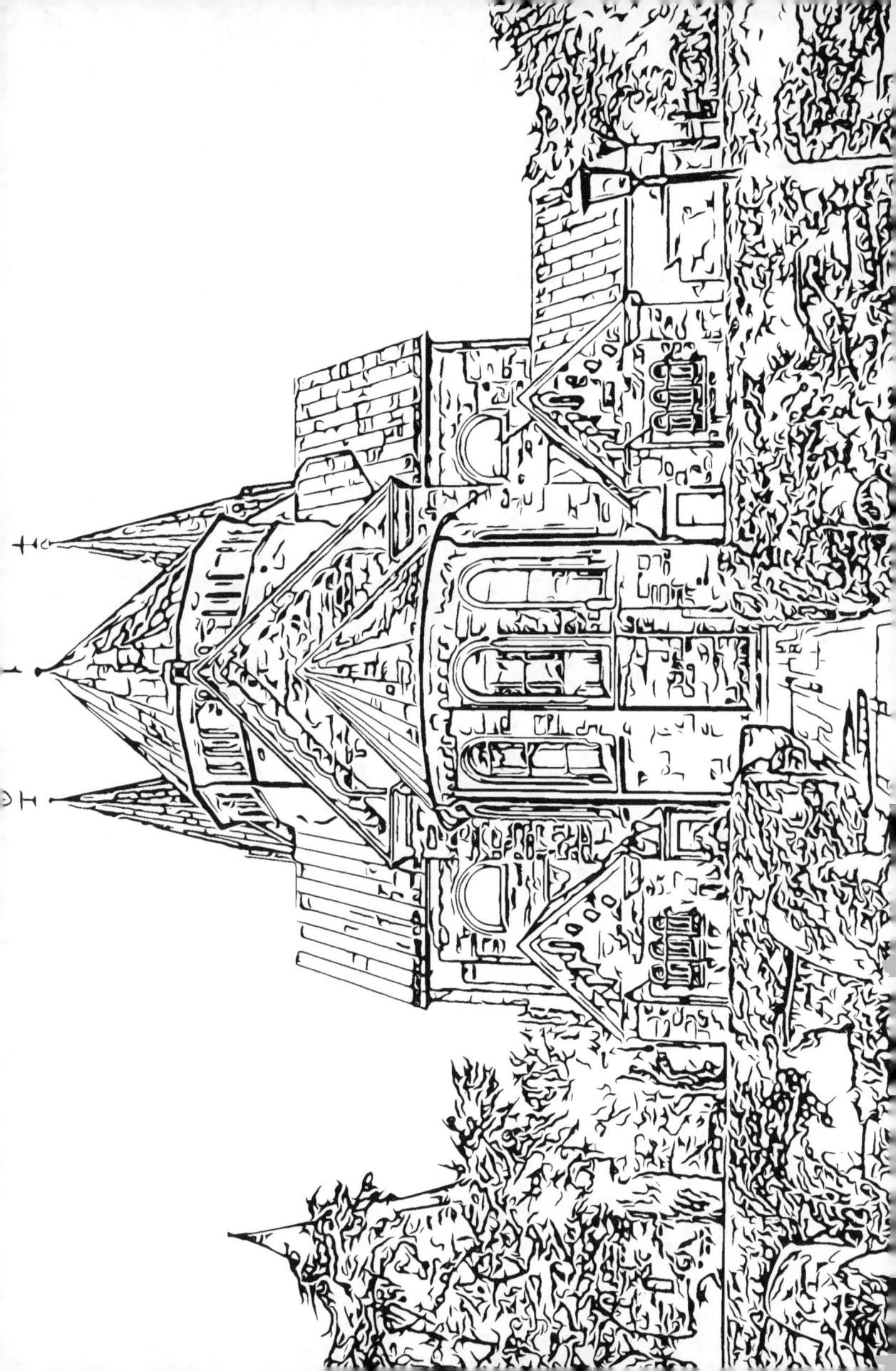

Harbor in the Mediteranean

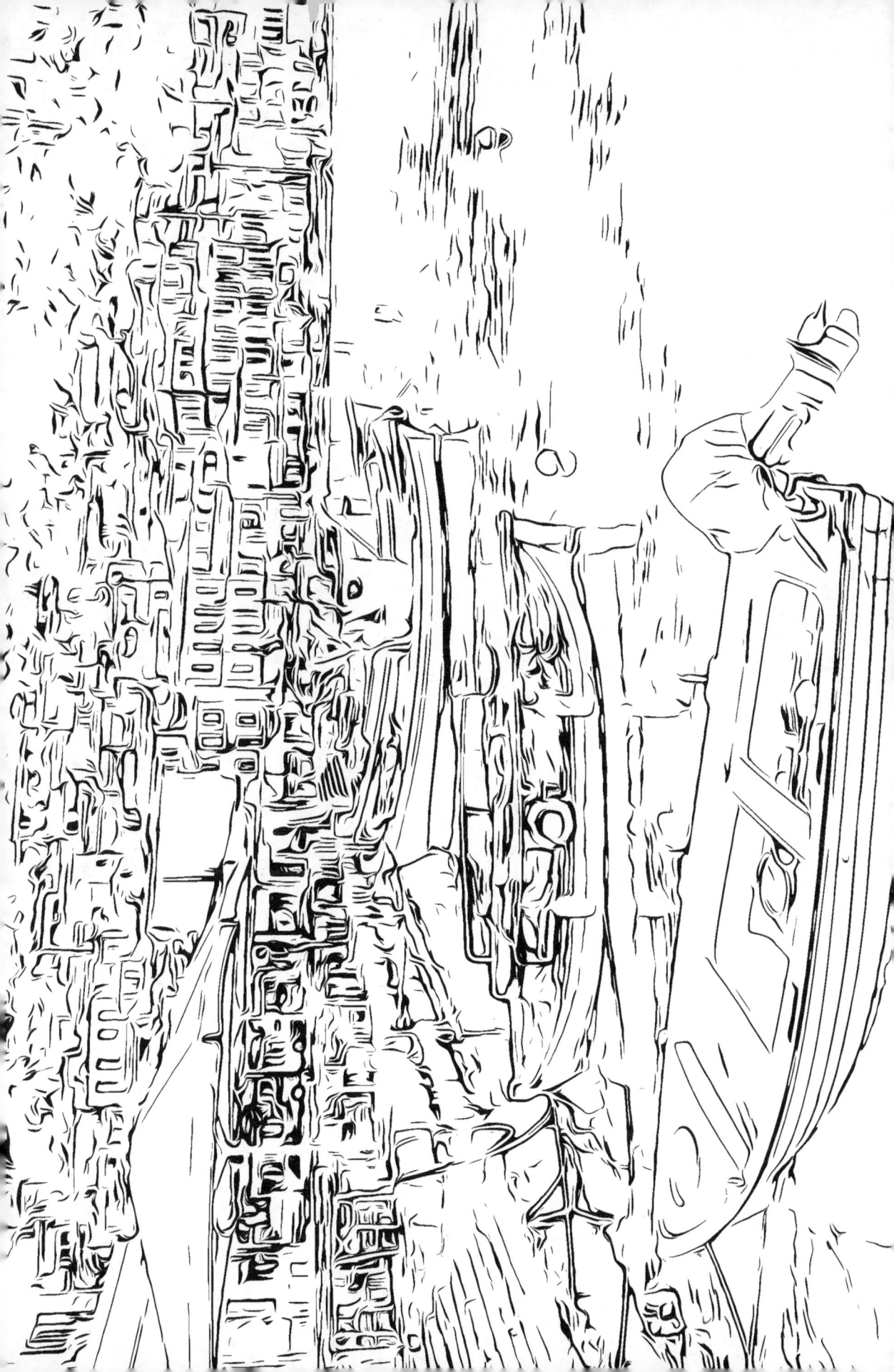

Monestary Ruin, France

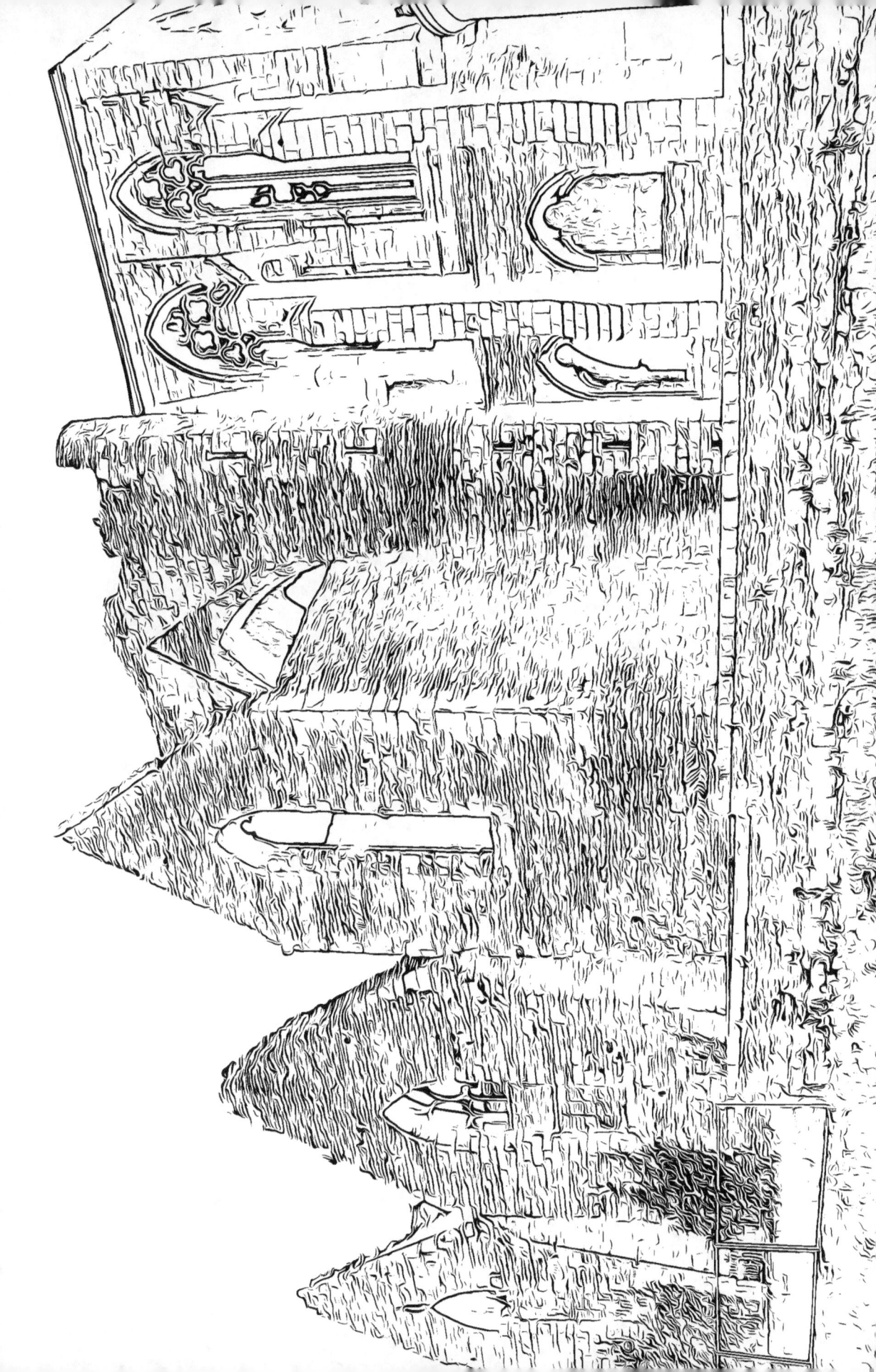

Monestary Ruin, France

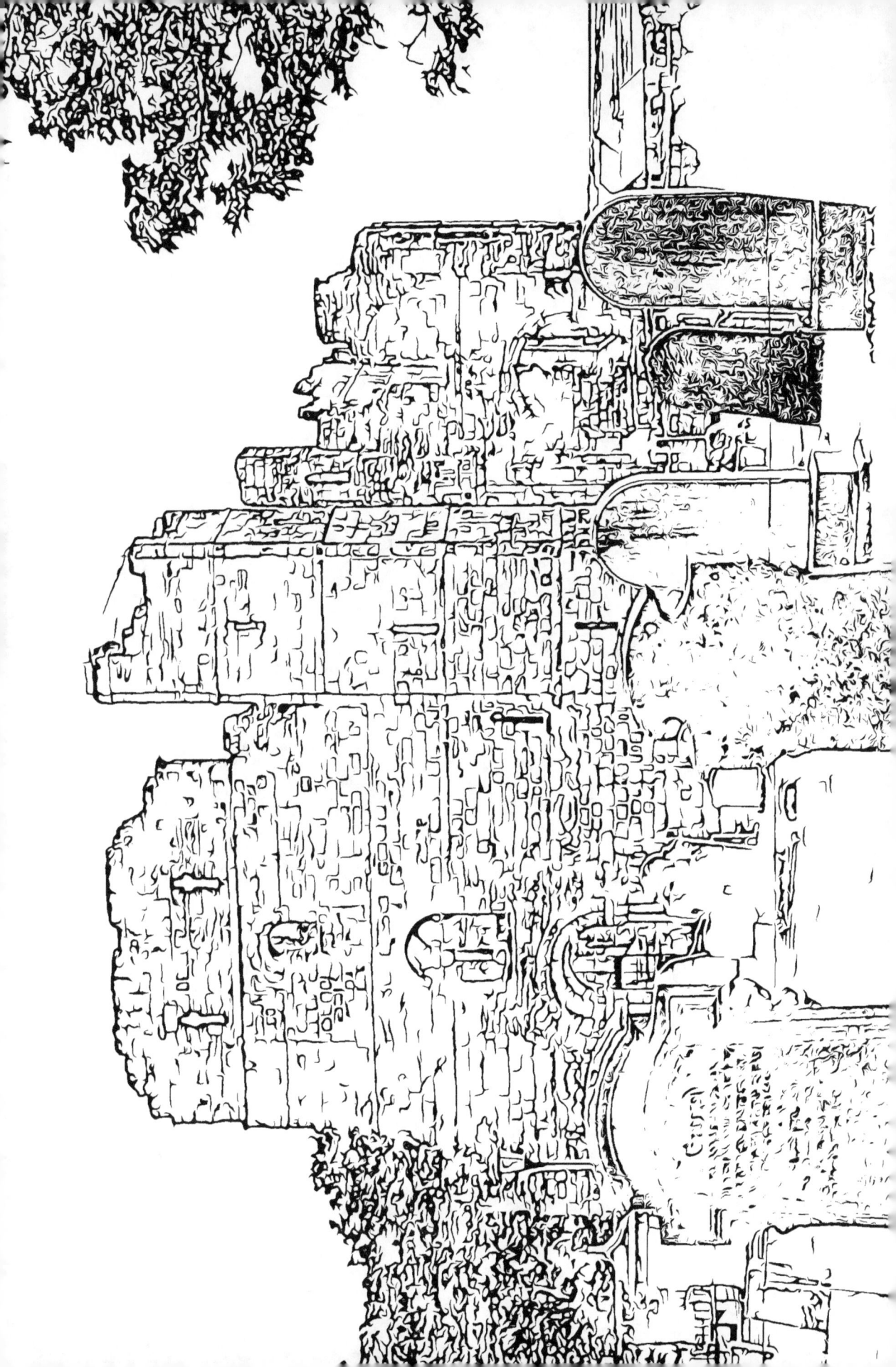

Mont Saint Michele, Normandy

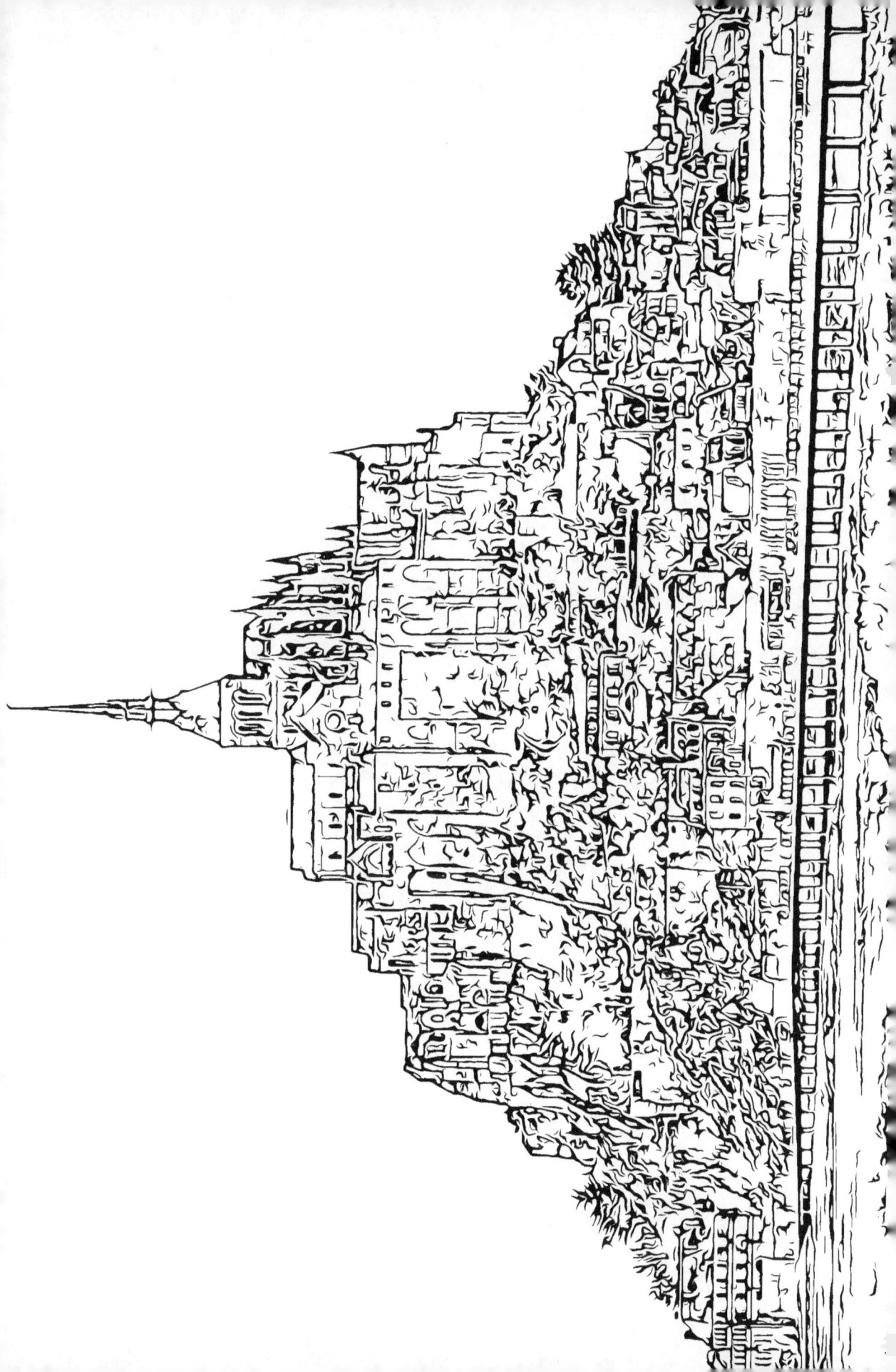

Arc de Triumph, Paris, France

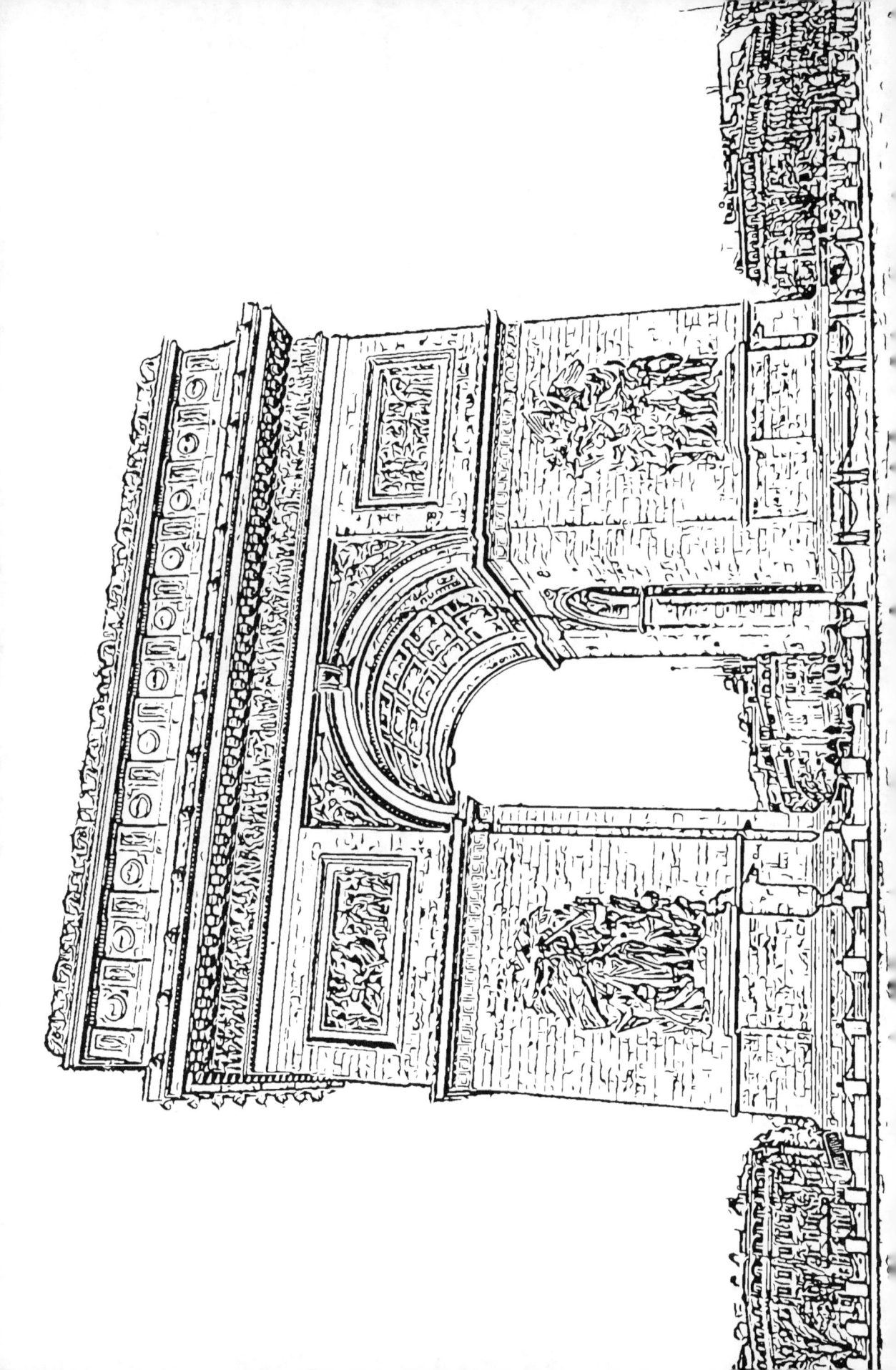

Pura Mandara Giri Semeru Agung, Indonesia

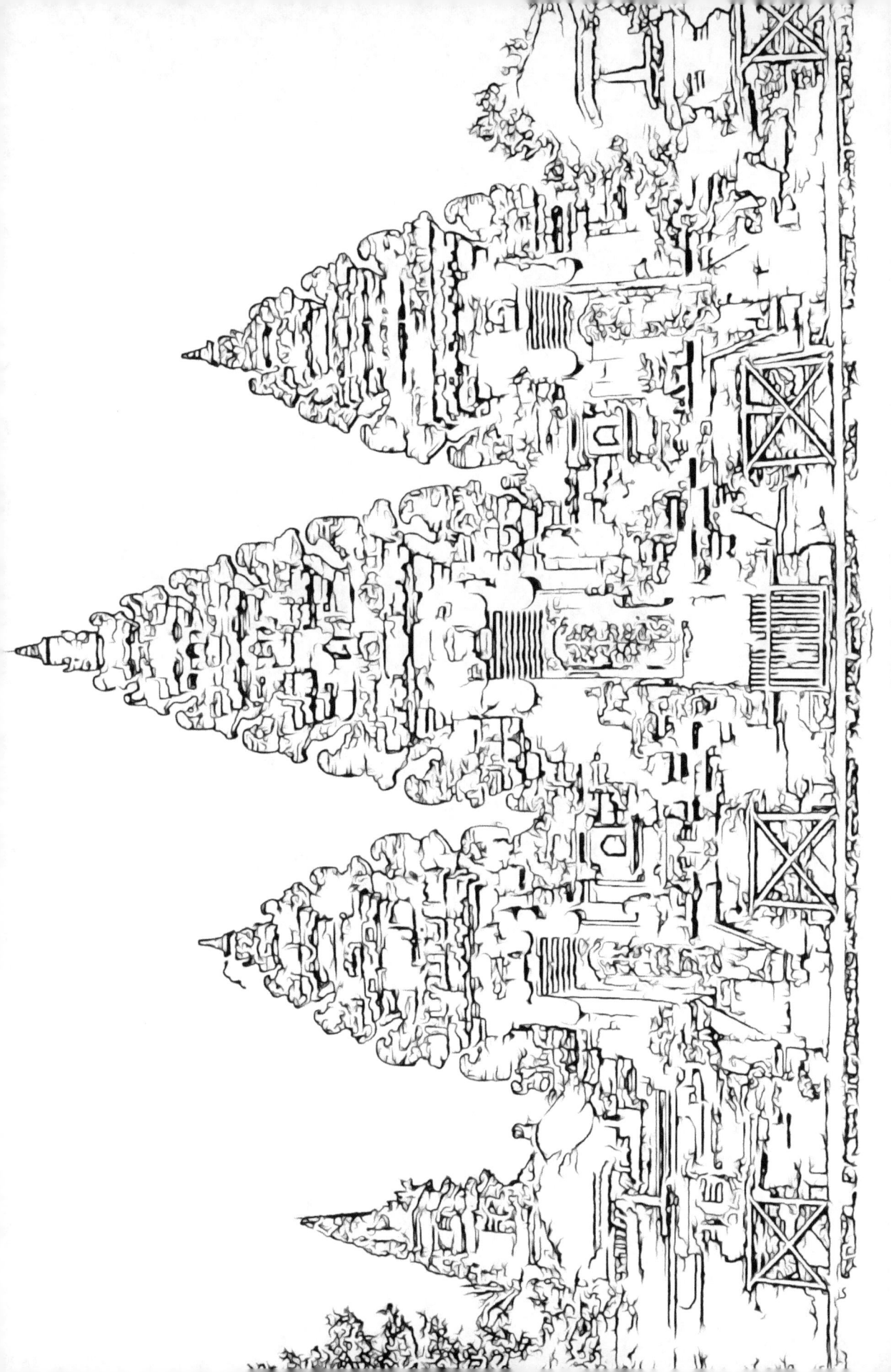

# Residence in Rome, Italy

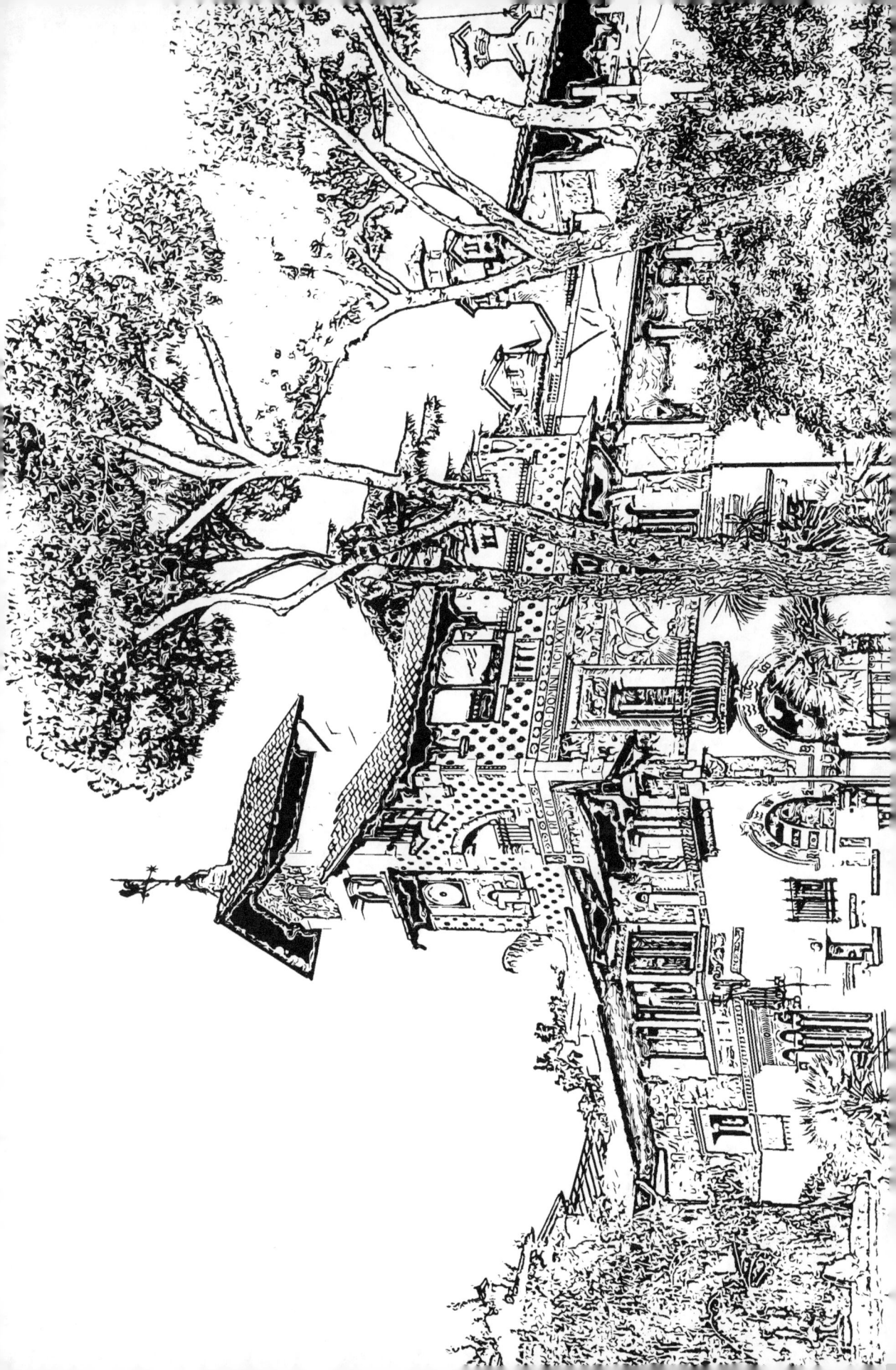

Rosette Church, New York City, New York

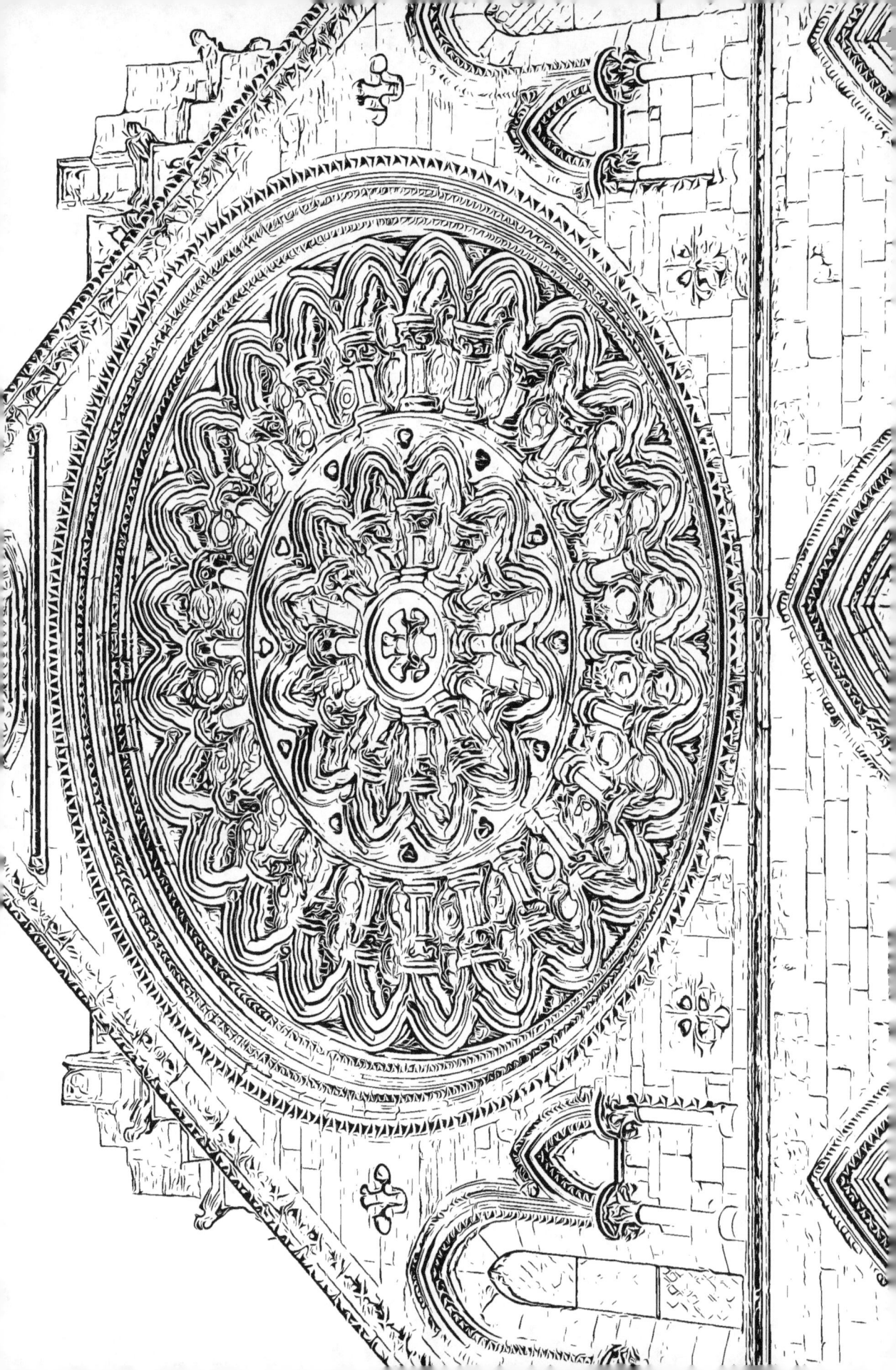

Ship in Brittany, France

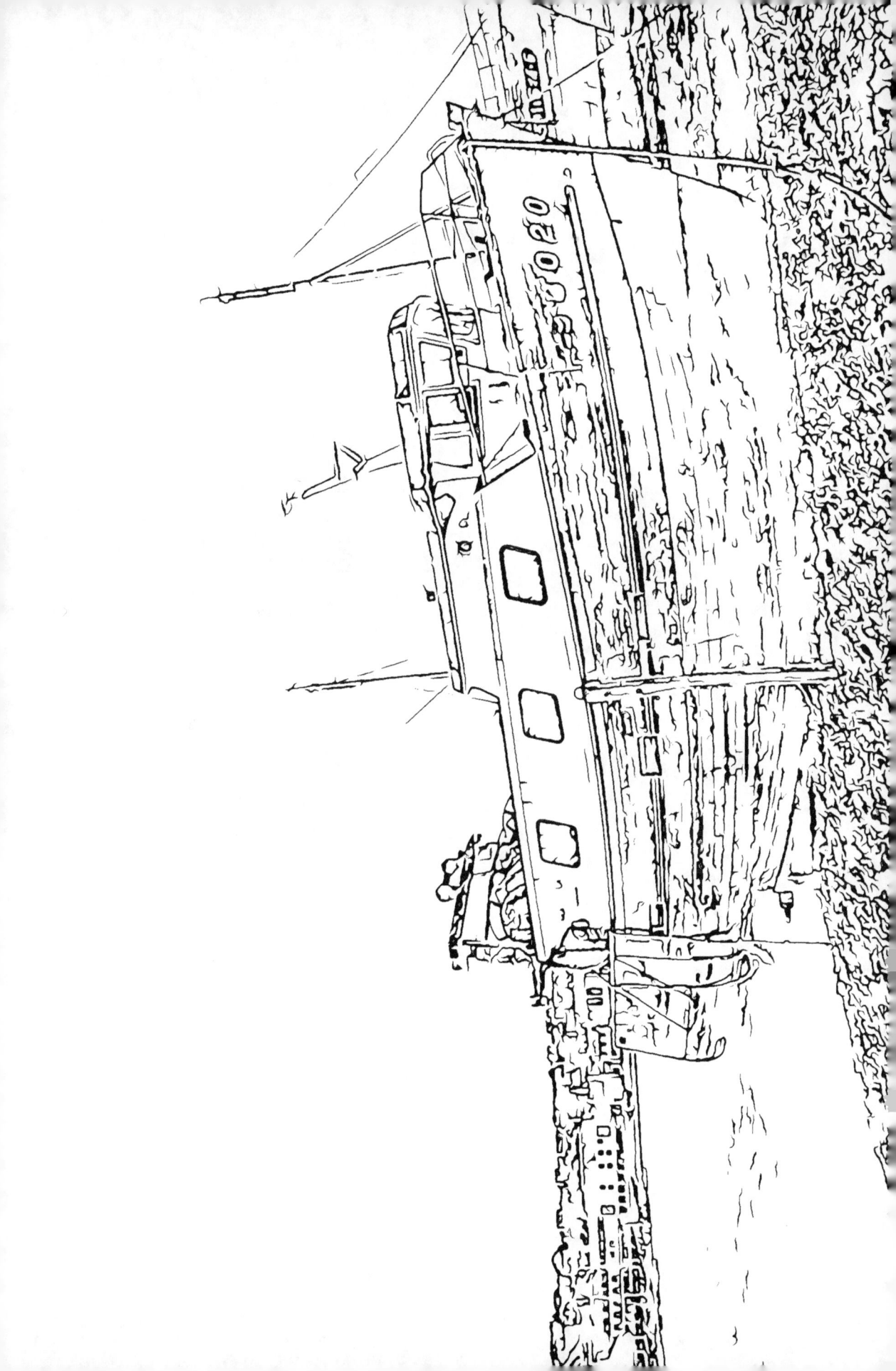

# Wooden Drawbridge

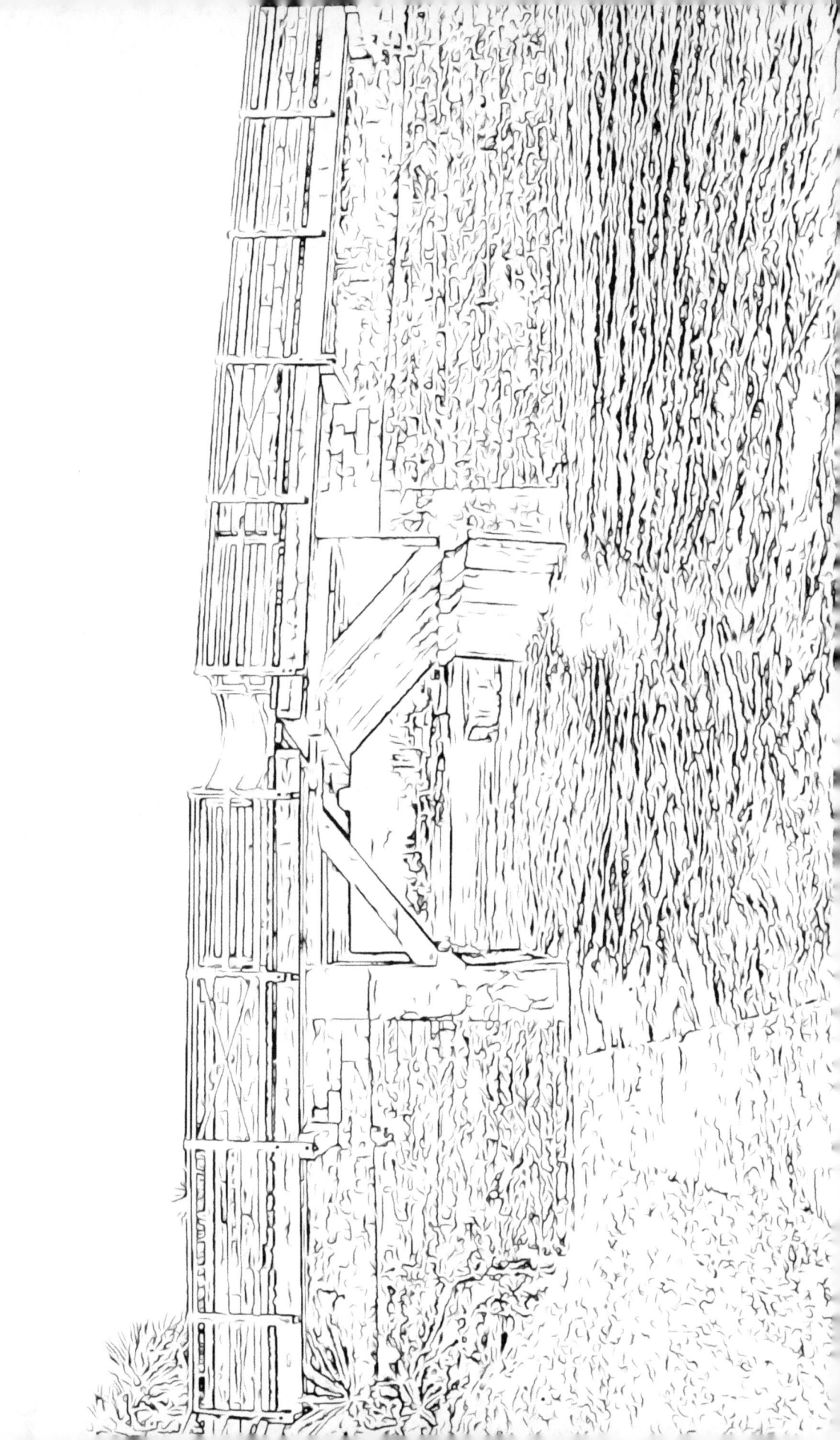

Village of Vernazza, Cinque Terre, Italy

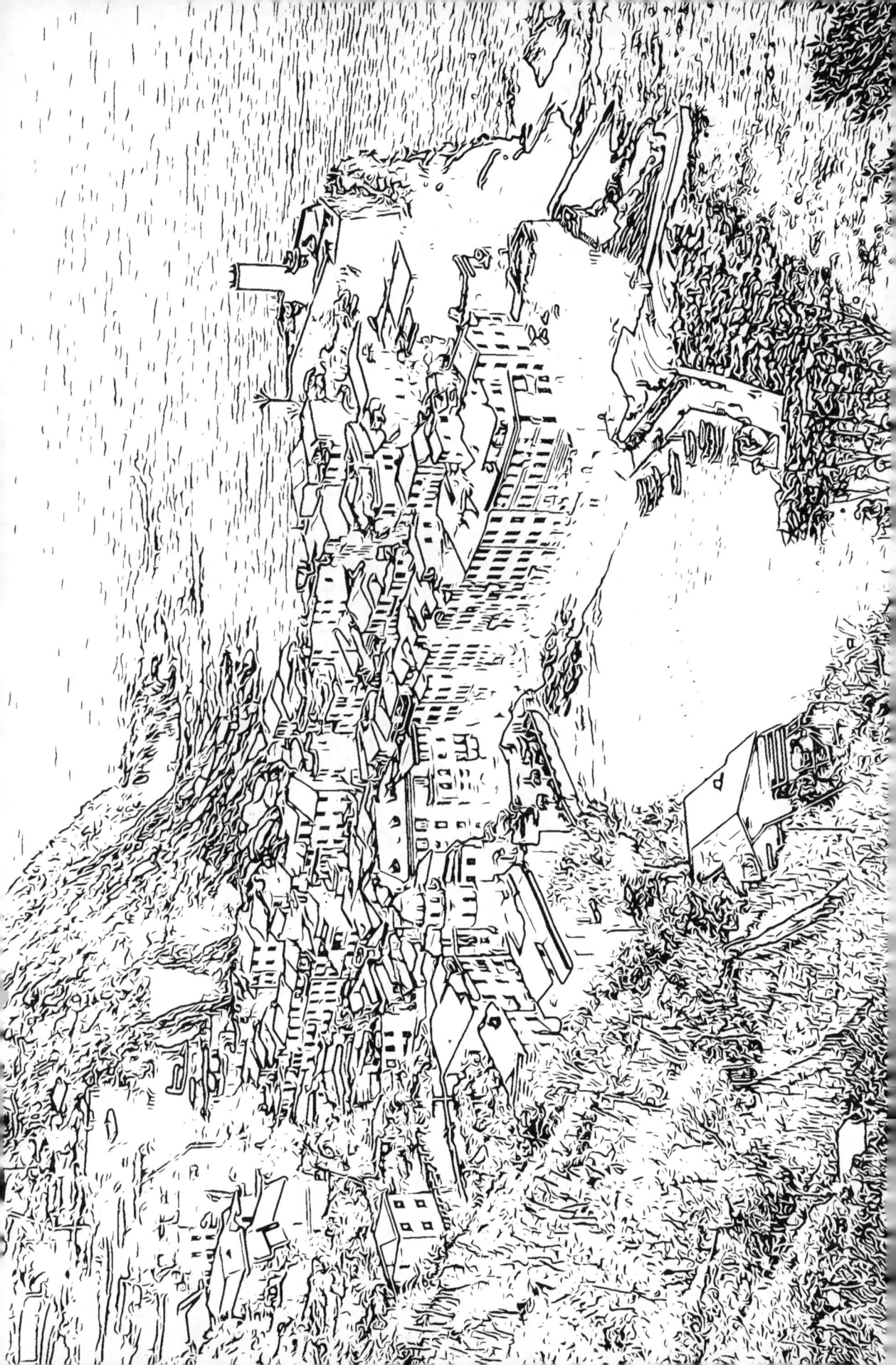

Birch Island, Sweden

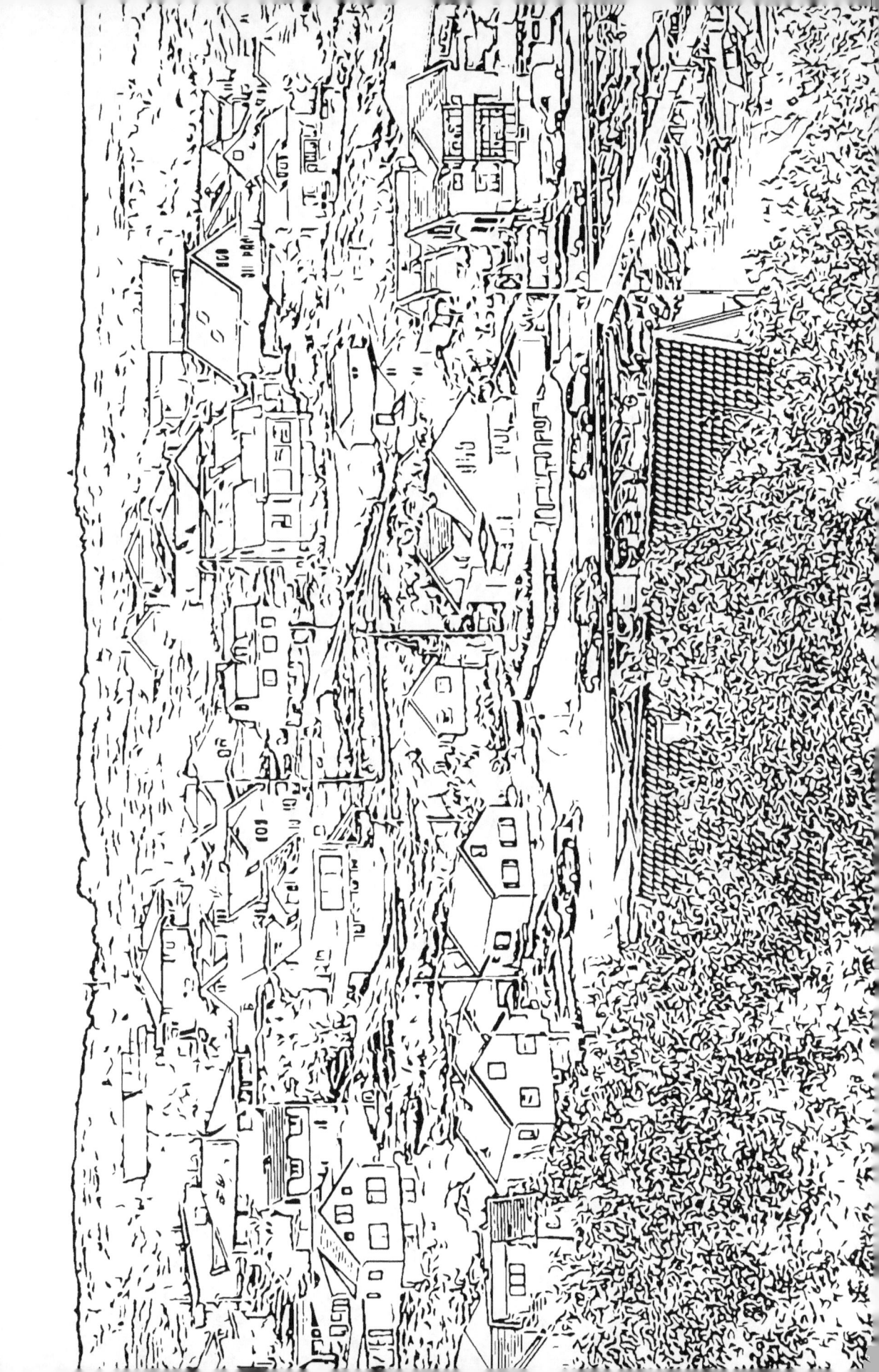

Random

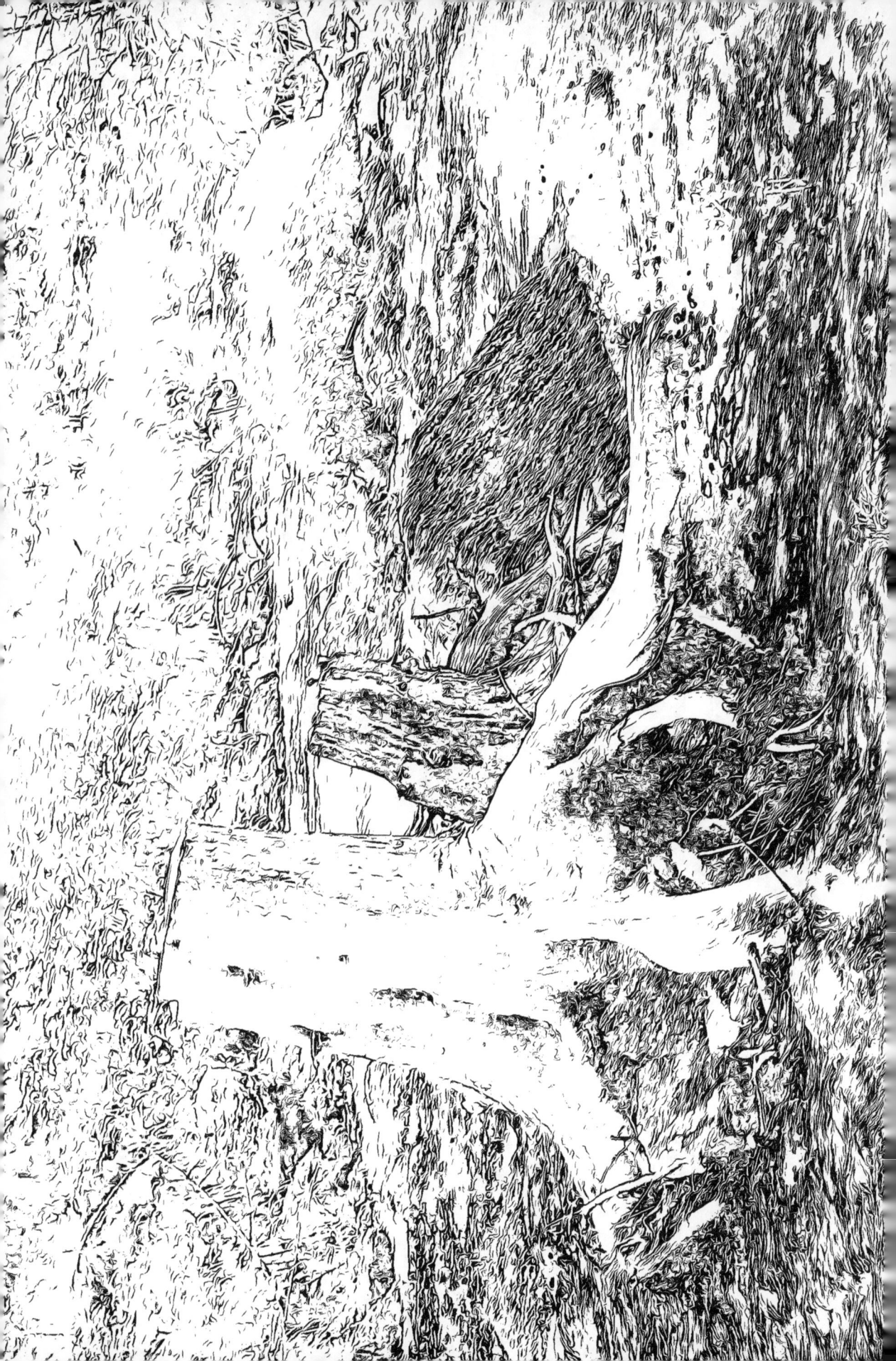

Vaulted Cellar in Rome, Italy

Thank You

www.ingramcontent.com/pod-product-compliance
Lightning Source LLC
Chambersburg PA
CBHW080538190526
45169CB00007B/2543